BACKPACKER'S
RECIPE
BOOK

BACKPACKER'S RECIPE BOOK

Inexpensive, Gourmet Cooking for the Backpacker

By

Steve Antell

PRUETT **P** PUBLISHING COMPANY

Boulder, Colorado

Library of Congress Cataloging in Publication Data

Antell, Steve, 1952-
  The backpacker's recipe book.

  Bibliography: p.
  Includes index.
  1. Outdoor cookery. 2. Backpacking.
I. Title.
TX823.A56   641.5'782   80-7569
ISBN 0-87108-549-6

Author photo courtesy of Farley Lewis
Illustrations by Cindy Ave' Lallemant

First Edition
       2   3   4   5   6   7   8   9

Printed in the United States of America

*I dedicate this book to my parents who first
introduced me to the mountains and have
understood my love of the outdoors since.*

Foreword

The idea of writing a backpacker's recipe book employing foods available only at a supermarket came to me in the woods six years ago. At that time, I did not know myself if it were possible to bring solely foods from a supermarket on a backpack trip, be within two pounds per person per day and still be nutritionally adequate. However, I began to gather ideas and write down recipes. Upon graduation from college, I devoted myself full time to the project—experimenting to create good-tasting, high-caloric, protein-containing foods, consulting with nutritionists, backpackers, and technical mountaineers, and learning how to write—the latter proving to be more difficult. For five months a year I worked exclusively on the project, using the remaining months in recuperation. Toward the end, my energy gave way and it was only with the constant prodding and encouragement of friends and my family that this book ever came into existence.

Many people offered their assistance in helping me write this book, particularly those listed below. Basic recipes for Ohm Balls and Coffee Toffee Bars came from Stacy Studebaker, Scotch Shortbread from Granny Kehoe, Biscuits from Cathy Hartman, and the Three-Minute Cookies recipe from Alice Antell. Teresa Trogdon gave her tea formula, Wendy Dows loaned me her Fruit Leather recipe, Tak Faojamera donated the Beef Jerky recipe, while Howard Weamer and Leslie Emerson offered some excellent backpack cooking ideas. I am deeply appreciative of nutritionists Barbara Smith, Colorado State University, and Nancy McKeeah, University of Colorado, for proofreading first drafts of my nutrition chapter and giving me reassurance in my understanding of nutrition.

Liz Taylor aided me in researching much needed technical information. Don Marquardt, Lynn Hammond, Dianna Cooke, and Claire Haley helped to proofread and edit the manuscript with Claire doing the majority of the work, including the typing. I am also grateful to Cindy Ave'Lallemant for her willingness to do the drawings on such short notice.

Finally, I thank many of my friends who not only ate what I cooked and offered constructive criticism and enthusiasm, but also accepted my inability to spend time with them while I was working on the manuscript. These people include Roger and Chrisy Almklov, Joe Frank, Cathy Hartman, Bruce Honisch, Vince Kehoe, Suzanne Murray, Felix Rigau, and Diane Russell.

Finally, I have tried to be as accurate as possible for all information contained within. Undoubtedly, human error does arise, no matter how careful one is. I would appreciate any mistake being brought to my attention.

Table of Contents

Introduction

This is a recipe book for backpackers who have been searching for an alternative method to eating outdoors other than the expensive, monotonous, soft, prepackaged, freeze-dried backpacking foods. The purpose of this book is to give recipes and suggestions to enable you to take foods only available from a grocery store on a backpack trip. What makes this recipe book unique among all other backpack cookbooks is that the food brought on a trip is designed to be within a weight limit of two pounds per person per day, satisfies all necessary nutritional requirements, is good tasting and practical to prepare and eat when traveling outdoors.

There are approximately eighty unique recipes in this book, covering areas of Breads, Bars and Candies, Meats, Dinners, Sauces, Spreads, Desserts, and Beverages. Included, too, are alternative procedures and ingredients to prepare many of these recipes in order to provide greater menu variety. A significant number of ideas and recommendations to formulating one's own recipes for backpack trips are also mentioned. In any type of cooking, knowledge of specific cookware and techniques is important. Consequently, short sections on both cookware and cooking techniques are included.

"What about this nutrition section?" you ask as you browse through the beginning part of this book. "Is this for one of those organic health enthusiasts?" My reply is that nutrition needs to be understood if one wants to adapt eating habits and foods to best fit his or her own environment when traveling outdoors and have the food within a reasonable weight limit of two pounds per person per day. Knowing about protein is necessary to use the many vegetable protein–source recipes

1

within and create one's own recipes while avoiding paying ridiculous exorbitant prices for freeze-dried meat.

Two years ago I wrote a complete book on the subject of backpack cookery. It took me three complete winters, four full revisions, and gave me a lot of headaches. The result was a book that read like a text—one that was extremely detailed, covering every facet of the subject from determining how many calories one needs as he grows older to ways of protecting one's food from animals. I realized later few people really need this much information in one source. Therefore, I resorted to writing this recipe book with short chapters on nutrition, cookware, and cooking techniques.

For those people unfamiliar with backpacking or just plain curious about food-related subjects, a bibliography is included that covers information like menu guides, ways to dry fruits and vegetables, selection of stoves, cooking gear to purchase, and how to build a fire.

This recipe book, then, is all about ways you can adapt food from the supermarket to bring on a backpack trip. Recipes and their variations and ideas to create one's own foods are given so as to be nutritionally adequate, good tasting, easy to prepare, and within two pounds per person per day. It is the expressed hope of the author that this book will be fun to use, shall improve your outdoor cooking in taste and pleasure, and reduce your food costs significantly.

Rye Crisp Package

Serving Size: 2 Triple Crackers   Protein: 1 gm.
Servings Per Container: 18   Carbohydrates: 9 gm.
Calories: 60   Fat: 1 gm.

Foods and Nutrition

An understanding of nutrition is a very important part of backpack cookery because it enables one to bring food weighing two pounds per person per day while meeting all nutritional requirements, satisfying personal tastes and is practical for outdoor preparation. In addition, knowledge of food composition will help you save money by wisely purchasing the most worthwhile foods and by planning a framework whereby you can formulate endless varieties of wholesome recipes.

Before beginning an actual discussion on foods and nutrition, a few explanatory notes are appropriate. It needs to be understood that nutrition is not an end in itself. If you are eating a nutritionally adequate diet, consuming different kinds or increased amounts of food types, like protein, will not markedly increase physical performance or make you healthier. The psychological factor of personal taste and food preference plays an important part in good eating and ought not to be underestimated. You can take along really nutritious food, but the food does no good if it is not eaten. For instance, going on an extended backpack trip without taking along specially pre-

3

pared freeze-dried or dehydrated individual foods is a new experience for many people. With these individuals, taking only foods suggested here might be a bad experience. It is suggested you change your eating habits slowly—mix new meals with freeze-dried until you become accustomed to the new tastes.

Many of the recipes given in this book use vegetable sources to fulfill protein requirements. Although these recipes are perfectly adequate from a nutritional standpoint, many people are in the habit of having meat for dinner and don't feel satisfied without it. I have, therefore, also included recipes that use dried meat that easily rehydrates in water. To satisfy personal tastes and cravings, though, you could easily bring along freeze-dried steaks or chops to supplement the many meatless meals.

Knowing what kinds of foods contain how many calories or grams of protein is valuable in order to minimize weight and maintain nutritionally adequate menus. I do not advocate the practice of always counting calories or grams of protein for all foods taken on a trip, or determining number of calories one will need when backpacking. However, one can check and obtain a good approximation of whether food taken is nutritionally adequate by quickly estimating nutritional values from several types of foods to be taken. To aid in this approximation, the appendix lists individual amounts of protein and calories of all recipes in this book. Included, too, are amounts of protein and calories per pound of foods commonly taken backpacking.

Calories

Since calories are our source of energy and heat, we need to have some idea of how many are needed on a trip. This number varies according to age, weight, height, activity, and air temperature; so an exact calculation is difficult. We can get a rough idea of our daily energy requirement, however, from the experiences of others. The National Outdoor Leadership School (NOLS), for instance, rations 3,750 calories per person per day on its 31-day summer expedition course. They increase the amount 20 percent, to 4,500 calories, for winter trips![1] This

---

[1]Nancy Pallister, ed., *NOLS Cookery*, p. 5-6, 1974.

figure is for young adults, in groups that are two-thirds male, one-third female. NOLS students participate in daily activities which are more physically strenuous and of longer duration than a person taking an easy day's hike in the hills.

Using NOLS' figure as a quick guide, you can increase the number of calories if you are especially large, going very long distances, hiking over rugged terrain, or carrying an exceptionally heavy pack; or decrease it when carrying small packs, doing more leisurely travel.

Let us use as your approximation for daily energy needs 3,600 calories per person per day for summer, and 4,320 calories for winter—knowing full well that energy demands vary greatly, and that these figures reflect activities of moderate intensity, like NOLS'. If one wishes to limit his food weight to two pounds per day, then the food taken must contain 1,800 calories per pound for summer, and 2,170 calories per pound for winter.

Initially it might appear easy to meet this arbitrary limit, for a pound of carbohydrate or protein contains 1,800 calories while fat contains 3,500 calories. Examining Appendix I, however, listing calories per pound of foods commonly taken backpacking, one notes that many food categories have fewer than 1,800 calories per pound—most beverages, cereals, fruits and vegetables, grain or flour products, sugar, canned meats, milk, many cheeses, instant sauce mixes, and soups. These foods are important and cannot be left at home for they comprise a backpacker's breakfast, part of his lunch, and dinner. In order to bring such foods and still have a low weight limit per day, it is necessary to compensate by bringing other foods having a higher caloric-per-weight ratio, which is fats. Examine Table I.

Table I

		Calories Per Pound	Useable Protein (gm.)
Cereals	Oatmeal, 1 minute	1760	42
	Granola, commercial	2080	≈29
	Granola (recipe)	2120	36
	New Cereal (recipe)	2190	37
	Wheatena	1620	≈28
Snacks	Bar recipes (average)	2200	24
	Hershey's chocolate bar	2430	≈22
Breads	Sweet Bread recipe (average)	1900	36
Crackers	Rye Crisp	2030	9
Soups-Sauces	Knorr	1950	≈23
Meat	Beef jerky	1600	86
	Granburger	1680	≈142
	Pemmican (recipe)	2630	≈45
	Tuna	1130	89
Dinners	Dinner recipes (average)	1820	39
Starch	Rice, white	1650	21
	Egg noodles	1760	35
	Instant potatoes	1650	≈20
	Sauces—thickener recipes (average)	1840	22
Spreads	Brown sugar	1690	0
	Honey	1380	0
	Oleomargarine	3270	≈0
	Peanut butter	2630	54
	Cheese, cheddar	1800	79
	Spreads recipes (average)	2330	49
Dried Fruit	Raisins	1330	≈8
	Apricots	1180	≈11
Drinks	Tang	1420	0
	Wylers	1920	0
	Milk, instant non-fat powdered	1630	133

Notice that commercial granola, the food many consider to be the ideal outdoor breakfast, has 2080 calories per pound. Granola is, therefore, acceptable for summer use but not quite for winter if one wants to be under two pounds per day. How can one lighten the amount of food taken and still meet daily energy requirements? For breakfasts the answer is to use margarine and eat other foods that are light in weight while containing a lot of bulk. Fats have more than twice as many calories per weight as carbohydrates and take longer to digest. Granola, when soaked in milk, does not expand. A cup of granola makes a cup of granola. Eating foods with bulk adds to the feeling of having a full meal. A cup of Wheat Hearts or oatmeal when cooked makes four cups and two cups of cereal, respectively. Thus, by eating Wheat Hearts or oatmeal with margarine for breakfast (providing you like it), food weight can be cut down, energy value increased, and overall bulk or actual eating quantity is maintained. (See new cereal recipe that contains 2190 calories per pound.) Similarly, for lunch, margarine or peanut butter on crackers or bread supplies needed calories with low weight. Pemmican is an ideal example of a rich food high in calories and low in weight that can be eaten for lunch. Dinners, which are composed mostly of starches, meat, and seasonings, may also be boosted in energy value by additional fats. The average energy values for recipes of breads, bars and candies, dinners, sauces—thickeners, and spreads are greater than 1800 calories per pound and demonstrate that fats added to food can make meals low in weight and still be good tasting.

Another technique whereby one can reduce food weight is simply not to take, substitute, or reduce in amounts foods that are low in caloric value. Classic examples of foods low in calories are dried fruit, canned goods, sugar, and Tang. For instance, most gorps contain a predominance of raisins; several pounds of raisins is unnecessary weight. If one plans to add dried fruit to a hot cereal, one can still get the fruit's taste and decrease the amount of fruit used by boiling the fruit in with the cereal. Sugar to sweeten cereals can be reduced by using a lesser amount of honey (honey being a lot sweeter than sugar) or artificial sweetener. The breakfast drink Tang weighs a lot for the amount of drink produced. Wylers weighs less, makes proportionately the same amount of drink, and produces the same amount of vitamin C as Tang. One may also bring alternative sources of needed protein which are higher in caloric content than canned meat, as discussed in the section of complementing proteins.

Until now, it has been understood that caloric intake ought to be equivalent to one's daily expenditures. What actually happens most of the time outdoors, however, is that daily energy requirements are greater than food intake, resulting in gradual weight loss. Some of this can be attributed to not having a large appetite when outdoors. A difference of 875 calories between energy needs and food intake causes a quarter pound of body fat to be metabolized. In summer, when it is warm, a quarter-pound loss of body weight per day for a week's trip is not too critical. Most of us can easily afford to lose two pounds of body fat. If, through experience, one feels comfortable on such a low caloric diet, then menus can be planned accordingly and food weight further lightened. However, it is prudent always to carry a reserve supply of food in case of emergencies or an unexpected occurrence. If the weight loss were to continue, though, for an extended period of time (three weeks or more), some people would begin to experience hunger. For short outings in winter, however, one has to be more careful about weight loss. A low summer diet of 3,000 calories consumed in winter would produce one-half pound of body fat loss a day. This energy deficit would probably result not only in hunger but in an uncomfortable inability to stay warm, especially while trying to sleep.

Carbohydrates

Nutritionists divide food into the categories of carbohydrates, fat, and protein. One gram of carbohydrate produces four calories, as opposed to four calories for protein and nine calories for fat. Carbohydrates are digested faster than either fats or protein. The average American consumes approximately 46 percent of his diet in carbohydrates.[2] Digestible carbohydrates are found primarily in the form of sugar and starches.

An advantage of eating carbohydrates for the backpacker is that consuming foods high in sugar gives quick energy when one is feeling tired. This is especially important late in the day

---

[2]*Recommended Dietary Allowances*, p. 34, National Academy of Sciences, 1974.

when one begins to feel the afternoon blahs. Eating a little bit of sugar at this time, like a candy bar or hard candy, does wonders. Carbohydrates have additional beneficial results at high altitudes. Climbers on expeditions (above 17,000 feet) tend to lose weight because at such elevation one does not have an appetite for fatty foods or meats. Sweets have always maintained their popularity at high elevations. For those experiencing a lack of appetite, or even a nauseated feeling when eating foods at high altitudes, a diet principally of carbohydrates aids in alleviating the problem.

Fats

Fats are an excellent source of energy for outdoor travelers who carry their own food because they are a concentrated source of energy. They also have a high satiety value, taking longer to digest that either carbohydrates or protein. One gram of fat produces over twice as many calories for the weight as either carbohydrates or proteins. Fats can be taken by backpackers in the form of oleomargarines or liquid oils for they will not turn rancid when kept unrefrigerated for long periods of time.

How much fat then should a backpacker take on a trip? While talking to a nutritionist I suggested 35 to 40 percent of one's total diet consist of fat when traveling outdoors. This is equivalent to three-fourths of a cup of margarine a day if margarine is the only form of fat for a 3,800-calorie per person per day diet. The nutritionist became absolutely aghast with such a recommendation. On such a "high-fat" diet I was supposedly going to get gallbladder problems and have all sorts of ugly difficulties—I am still waiting for this to happen. Other nutritionists later confirmed my convictions that one ought to be able to consume as little or as much fat as desired, provided of course that one does not exceed his body's caloric requirements and is physically very active.[3] At high altitudes,

---

[3]One must have at least 1 to 2 percent of one's daily energy intake in the form of fats to obtain some essential fatty acids which the body needs. Clinical studies have indicated that exercise promotes the oxidation of fats (Ernst Jokl, *Nutrition Exercise and Body Composition*, pp. 14, 16). It is generally considered that an intake of unsaturated fats (fats from vegetable sources) rather than saturated fats (from animal sources) reduces one's susceptibility to atherosclerosis.

though, above 12,000 to 14,000 feet, the intake of fats ought to be reduced because it severely interferes with acclimatization.[4]

Now three-fourths of a cup of margarine per person per day is a bit extreme. However, most of us do eat this amount of fat (the average American diet consists of eating 42 percent fats)[5] in our daily diet, though not solely in the form of margarine. Fats in our daily diet also include sources from meats, salad dressings, and dairy products. It has been the author's experience that on a typical summer backpack trip, people consume only 15 to 20 percent of their total diet in fats. Admittedly, this low percentage figure has a lot to do with personal tastes, for on a hot summer day one does not have a real craving to eat fats. In winter one desires a greater percentage of fats in one's diet. The trick is to discover ways to make food to be good tasting and be high in fats along with finding out what one's fat taste tolerances are. Carrying a spread for breads or crackers consisting of peanut butter or margarine (or butter) mixed with a bit of honey is one way to have a high intake of good-tasting, fat-containing foods.

Proteins

Proteins are one of the most complex biological substances. They are composed of amino acids and are the basis of every part of our cells, muscles, blood, nerves, tendons, and enzymes of our body, and can be derived from both animal and vegetable sources. Animal protein includes meat, milk, and egg products. Vegetable protein is similar to animal protein, differing only in quantity and quality. Vegetable protein sources include whole grains, legumes (peas, beans, lentils) and nuts.

There are two important facts concerning the metabolism of proteins. First, proteins are not stored to any appreciable extent. If proteins are consumed in quantities greater than is needed for tissue repair, such protein (amino acids) will be ultimately converted to glycogen. This glycogen will be stored as fat if the caloric portion of the diet has been met. Thus, a day's supply of protein ought to be eaten during periods spaced

---

[4]The metabolism of fats requires more oxygen than for that of carbohydrates or proteins.

[5]*Recommended Dietary Allowances*, p. 33, National Academy of Sciences, 1974.

throughout the day, not all at once. Secondly, if protein is eaten when the caloric requirements have not been satisfied through an adequate intake of fats and carbohydrates, the protein will be converted to glucose (4 cal/gm.) to fulfill the body's energy needs. Therefore, one should supplement even a snack of protein, a quart of milk or part of a meat bar, for example, with some other energy-yielding food to gain the protein's full nutritive value.

To answer the question how much protein does one need? One first has to understand how protein amounts are measured. Our standard of protein measurement will be Useable Protein, the protein that is fully available to the body as a protein source. A food having a high percentage of Useable Protein per total weight is a good protein source. Three interrelated factors influencing Useable Protein are the quality, quantity, and digestibility of protein. One cannot have a good protein source and be deficient in any one of these three factors. A 154-pound male needs approximately 43 grams of Useable Protein per day, while a 128-pound woman needs 36 grams of Useable Protein per day.[6]

Net Protein Utilization (NPU) has been calculated to indicate the percentage of Useable Protein in a given food.[7] NPU figures for animal protein range from 60 to 94 percent. Protein from vegetable sources are less, having an NPU of 30 to 60 percent. These low figures reflect a deficiency in certain amino acids essential to the body. There is a way, though, to eat vegetable protein so one can meet protein requirements. This is accomplished by complementing one food source's amino acids with other amino acids. For instance, peanut butter and powdered milk (high in calories) complement one another so that all the amino acids needed by the body to manufacture new proteins are present.[8] In this book, the majority of recipes, especially those that use exclusively vegetable protein for their protein source, are complemented to increase the amount of Useable Protein available.

---

[6]Frances Moore Lappe, *Diet For A Small Planet*, p. 45, 1971, lists such NPU values.

[7]Ibid.

[8]Ibid. p. 80.

The discussion so far has been limited to amounts of protein. What are some good sources of protein? In backpacking, animal protein has been the traditional way of fulfilling protein requirements. This makes sense because animal protein has the highest percentage of Useable Protein versus overall food weight (high NPU value). Animal protein sources include eggs and meat along with dairy products like milk and cheese. Milk and eggs can be bought dehydrated and have NPU values of 62 and 83, respectively. Taking meat on a trip as a protein source presents problems, however, because of its high cost and susceptibility to spoilage. With the advent of freeze-dried meat, spoilage is no longer a problem, but financial costs still are. During cold winter months, one can bring freshly-cooked meat on an outdoor trip since cold weather inhibits any bacterial growth. For weekend trips, one can bring canned meats like tuna, chicken, ham, etc. On longer excursions, canned meats are no longer feasible because of weight restrictions. For example, canned tuna has 1130 calories per pound (see Table I). This is when many of us carry specially prepared meat bars and freeze-dried meats like steaks, chops, or hamburger. These foods satisfy the backpacker's requirements of lightness in weight and high protein without spoilage. Freeze-dried meats are appealing to lots of people, but there are alternative sources of animal protein that are much less expensive and are excellent for backpacking, too. These include beef jerky, dried salted meat and pemmican (from recipe), salami, bacon bits, hard cheeses, and milk.

Vegetable proteins can also be an important source of nutrients for the backpacker and frequently contain more than 1800 calories per pound, which is the criterion for maintaining a two-pound-per-person weight limit per day, as previously mentioned. Flours, nuts, and seeds can be baked into an endless variety of dense breads, sweet bars, candies, and cereals, whose ingredients are complemented! Dense breads or sweet bars made from the recipes within contain 1900 and 2200 calories per pound, respectively and supply more than enough protein per day.[9] These pre-baked foods and prepared bread mixes can also help eliminate the monotony of backpack eating

---

[9]Breads can be baked adding little or no water; almost all the moisture comes from energy-containing liquids like honey or margarine and eggs.

on extended outings or on frequent trips. Texturized soy protein products are the other source of vegetable protein for the backpacker. Soy foods look and taste like real meat and are nutritious and inexpensive. They are great to add to meatless dinners. Texturized soy products currently on the market today are soy burger, bacon, and meat bits. In the near future, chicken- and ham-flavored soy cubes might become commercially available.

Getting enough protein on a backpack trip ought not to be a major concern if one plans foods which include some of the richer protein foods mentioned above. Appendix I lists most of these foods and their amounts of Useable Protein. Notice that milk, cheese, peanut butter, dried meats, "soy burger," and the recipes for cereals and breads are very high in protein. It is very easy to adapt a menu to contain more protein without a substantial increase in weight. For instance, a one-quart package of non-fat powdered milk supplies 60 percent of one's daily protein requirements. The milk powder weighs and costs approximately the same as an equivalent amount of Tang or Wylers. The recipes within for sweet bars contain a lot more protein than a candy bar. Sweet bars also add a lot more variety to one's menu. There are, then, good sources of protein for the backpacker besides freeze-dried meat. And some of these complemented sources of protein contain more than 1800 calories per pound.

Water and Salt

The correct amounts of water and salt are important concerns to backpackers because too much or too little will lead to immediate physical reactions such as weakness, fatigue, nausea, cramps, or even errors in judgment. Gross imbalances even lead to such serious consequences as heat exhaustion, heat stroke, and heat cramps. The body has a device for regulating the balance of water and salt, which usually works well enough in sedentary home life; but when we exercise a lot outdoors, salt and water demands increase, and if we do not meet these demands, we can be in trouble.

The two signs which indicate that one needs water are thirst and perspiration. Ignoring both warnings is asking for trouble. Free access to water is essential when the body demands it, since it is impossible to train the body to do without water.[10] One should anticipate drinking three to four quarts of water per day when backpacking during the summer. Some of this can be consumed by drinking tea, hot soup, or other beverages before dinner.

Water loss is always associated with salt depletion. A good rule of thumb for backpackers is to salt their meals at breakfast and dinner in the same proportions as when at home. For lunch, one receives salt by consuming such foods as peanuts, crackers, and margarine. Obtaining salt in this fashion normally ensures a proper salt intake. However, if water loss exceeds three and a half quarts per day, extra salt is needed. Two grams of salt per extra quart of water loss is recommended—approximately four salt tablets or one teaspoon of salt.[11]

Vitamins

The subject of vitamins is a touchy one for many individuals involving quite a few unsubstantiated prejudices. Nutritionists have divided foods into seven nutritional categories: milk, meat, dark green or deep yellow vegetables, citrus fruits, other fruits and vegetables, breads, and fats. A person is advised to eat a certain amount of food in each of these categories every day to obtain all the vitamins he needs. On backpacking trips, where meat, fresh vegetables, and fruits are usually not available, it would appear that serious vitamin deficiencies would soon become apparent. However, most foods taken backpacking do contain essential vitamins.

For weekend trips and outings up to several weeks in duration, vitamin concerns are needless. If one is out on a three-month expedition or takes many week-long trips throughout the whole summer, the taking of vitamin supplements is suggested. Such vitamin supplements ought to be broad in spectrum, containing eight to 12 vitamins. High dosages of two or three specific vitamins is not recommended because vitamin deficiency sometimes is inter-related with the lack of several

---

[10]*Recommended Dietary Allowances,* p. 23, National Academy of Sciences, 1974.

[11]Ibid. p. 90.

vitamins, and taking too much of one specific vitamin actually can be harmful.

Minerals

Minerals, the inorganic substances of the body, play an important role in the body's physiological functions. The actual amount of minerals the body requires each day is small (approximately three grams or less). Most backpacking foods contain the major mineral elements. Calcium actually is the only major mineral element one has to be concerned about. Three-fourths of a quart of milk per day or four ounces of cheese supplies the body's daily calcium requirement.

Trace elements are also needed by the body. Trace elements are minerals used in extremely minute amounts, down to limits of detectability. Outdoors one need only concern himself with iodine and iron requirements. Fulfilling one's salt requirement with iodized salt ensures that iodine requirements have been met. Iron is found in foods such as meat, eggs, vegetables, and fruits. However, for many people, especially growing children and women, iron intake is inadequate. The author suggests iron supplements for all persons on any extended outdoor trip. Many multiple vitamin pills contain iron.

*"The worst passion we mortals cherish
is the desire to possess."*

—D. T. Suzuki

Cookware

Specialized equipment is necessary for any kind of outdoor activity, and backpack cookery is no exception. Decisions to take equipment depend on many variables including number of people, types of food eaten, length of trip, and conditions expected. When in doubt of what to bring, it is better to err by bringing too few utensils than too many. Listed here are the different kinds of eating and cooking utensils that are needed and used outdoors. Little attempt has been made to discuss how equipment works or to compare different brands or designs of cooking gear. For such information, it is best to refer to a book on backpacking equipment.

Eating Utensils

Each person should bring a spoon, cup, and bowl. The spoon when combined with a pocketknife (which one should always carry in the outdoors) will take the place of a fork and eating knife. There are more choices in cups. Plastic cups are convenient, for they retain heat well and won't burn hands. A metal cup, with a thick lip at the top to prevent one's lips from burning, is nice because one can cook in it. Whichever cup is taken, plastic or metal, one should know how much his or her cup holds to facilitate cooking measurements. Individual markings can be placed on a cup by scratching or marking with a felt pen to give great accuracy. Bringing a bowl gives one a container to eat from and frees the cup for drinking at meals; bowls are also more versatile than plates.

Cooking Utensils

A big metal or wooden spoon is useful if one is cooking with large pots for a great number of people. It is especially important that it have a stout handle so it won't break when stirring thick foods. On a trip with two or three people, an oversized personal spoon suffices. A spatula is a must for any serious frying. Bringing a ladle along is only necessary when serving many hungry people. Whisks are great for mixing or whipping things but so is a short, stout, branched twig or a wide-mouth water bottle. On almost all trips a can opener is essential. If your pocketknife does not have one, a lightweight G.I. can opener can be bought at a backpack store. Pot grippers are not essential but they make handling hot items a lot easier. I use an ample supply of kitchen matches to start my fires or stove, but lightweight disposable lighters also work. The other item which is nice to have outdoors is a tea ball—a hollow, perforated, metal ball used to contain leaves when making tea.

The number and size of cooking pots and pans to bring on a trip depends on the size of the party and the types of food to be cooked. I personally bring the minimum amount of pots in order to save on weight. The largest pot ought to be capable of holding at least one pint for every person on the trip. Thus, a two-quart pot is sufficient for a group of three. The pot should have a tightfitting lid too because at high altitudes foods dry out rapidly. A lid also quickens cooking time, protects food from foreign matter, and can be used as a frying pan or another mixing bowl. Having a smaller, secondary pot that fits inside the larger pot is convenient for it can be used to make another course or hold hot drinks.

A pot or pan taken outdoors should be constructed out of aluminum, well made, and without fixed handles. Sometimes one can find such a pot at a thrift shop or army surplus store. These pots might not be out of thin gauge, lightweight aluminum, but their durability more than compensates for the little bit of extra weight one has to carry. Specially constructed cooksets with pots nestled neatly inside one another may be purchased at a camping goods store. There are also pot sets whereby the pots can stack on top of each other, the upper rim of one pot supporting the bottom of another pot. Stacked pots can be used as a double boiler or will keep one food warm while other food in the lower pot is cooking. Manufacturers of cooksets suitable for backpacking include Sigg, Optimus, Sven, Macro, along with many others.

Other cooking items to think about bringing are frying pans, bread pans, pie tins, bakery ovens, grills, and pressure cookers. Special lightweight frying pans made of aluminum with Teflon coating and a removable lid are available (8 ounces for a 7½ inch pan). If I plan to do much baking, I sometimes bring a lightweight bread pan (2½ ounces for a 2½ by 3½ by 6 inch pan) or a sturdy pie tin. For those desiring to be more extravagant, Optimus even makes a special baking oven designed for stove-top use. Pressure cookers have been made light enough to entice backpackers to buy them. They are most useful at high elevations where they can decrease cooking time. I naively took such a pressure cooker once on a five-day mountaineering trip. With all the climbing gear we brought, carrying the pressure cooker was an exercise in sheer madness (weight: 3 pounds). Finally, there are metal grills constructed out of hollow stainless steel tubing that make cooking over a fire a lot easier.

Storage Containers

Most foods taken outdoors are stored in polyethylene containers, which come in a variety of shapes and sizes. A one-quart, wide-mouth polybottle with a screw lid is one item I always take with me and recommend because it not only serves as a canteen but also doubles as a mixing container for powdered mixes like milk or pudding. Narrow-mouth polybottles also make excellent containers for long-term storage of liquids like cooking oil. If I bring more than a pound of margarine with me, I put it in a screw capped wide-mouth polyethylene container that has an opening big enough to insert a spoon. Collapsible plastic water bags are very useful for large groups, hold up to five gallons of water, and are light in weight.

The problem with using polyethylene containers is that they tend to retain odors and tastes. This difficulty is minimized by rinsing them out immediately after use or when carrying drinkable liquids, using an odor-free anodized aluminum bottle. Also, a polybottle or any other container sometimes leak; so if oil is being carried, it is wise to double-sack the container in plastic bags.

There is an endless variety of containers for storing spices, spreads, and condiments. One should avoid taking too many containers, for container weight and sizes quickly add up and most containers need to be carried for the duration of the trip. I keep my spices in 35mm film cans. Plastic round fishing egg containers that are transparent and can be stacked on top of one another by screwing together work well also. Salt and pepper are usually carried in plastic shakers because the small cardboard containers they come in at the store collapse under any pressure and disintegrate when wet. Tiny amounts of liquids like vanilla or rum extracts fit well in small polyethylene containers with a gasket screw lid, while liquid soap can be carried in little plastic shampoo bottles with a flip-lock lid. The safest container I have found in which to store syrups and honey are empty plastic mustard squeeze bottles. These containers are constructed out of tough plastics and have screwcap openings that cannot be lost or accidentally opened. Jams, jellies, peanut butter, margarine, or other spreads may be kept in flat, plastic, round tins with a heavy-threaded lid. Plastic tins allow easy access to substances within and still are quite safe from leaks. Crush-proof, lightweight empty potato chip canisters are excellent containers for carrying round-shaped crackers.

Plastic bags are what most foods are stored and carried in when traveling outdoors. Plastic bags are light in weight, inexpensive, waterproof, and are easily labeled. Surprisingly enough, the toughest bags I have found to keep foods in are empty bread bags or the free produce bags from the grocery store. Freezer bags work well too but are expensive. I don't like regular sandwich bags, for their bottom seams always seem to split open. Zip-lock closure bags eliminate closure clasps, but maintaining a seal frequently is a problem. If one is packing food for a large expedition, outdoor program, or many trips, the use of heat-sealed bags ought to be considered. These are thick plastic bags with the openings permanently sealed by an iron. The only way to open the bag is to puncture it. Heat-sealed bags are ideal for pre-made mixes of foods to be eaten during one sitting.

Kerosene or white gas fuel brought backpacking ought to be stored in a leak-proof, non-corrosive metal container with a gasket on the lid. Sigg makes such an aluminum bottle. Fuel containers should be clearly labeled to prevent any possible confusion. A small funnel or pouring cap can be carried to assist in the refilling of white gas or kerosene stoves.

Fires and Stoves

When there are no restrictions against fires, backpackers have a choice between a fire and a stove for cooking. Each has its advantages over the other. A stove may always be used to cook over but there are many specific instances when a fire cannot or should not be used. Fires require much time and effort to build. The whole process is made more difficult, if not impossible, when it is rainy, snowy, or windy outside. Cooking fires should not be built in areas with little or no wood, like a heavily visited camping site or populated mountain areas. This is especially true in sub-alpine and alpine regions where vegetation is extremely sparse and takes many years to grow, and decomposed wood is needed to provide minerals and a substrate for new forms of plant life to grow in. Evidence of a cooking fire here would remain for hundreds of years. Before going on a trip, it is best to check with National Park or U.S. Forestry officials to see if fire permits are required, and if there are areas where fires are not allowed. If time, weather, and environment allow, I usually cook over a fire. Otherwise, I always use my stove. It is not uncommon during a summer trip to use both. As will become apparent when one is outdoors, if one plans to do backpacking or outdoor traveling to any extent, having a stove is mandatory. One just has to be aware of when a fire can or can not be used.

Backpacking stoves come in many shapes, designs, and makes. Name brands include Svea, Optimus, Phoebus, Gaz Blevet, MSR, Coleman, and Gerry. A typical white gas backpacking stove weighs a little under two pounds and burns about a third of a pint of gas per person per day. Other stoves burn liquid petroleum gas or kerosene. Modern-day backpacking stoves have been designed so that almost anybody would have little or no problem using them. Cooking on a stove is easy and convenient, which more than compensates for the stove's extra weight and possible mechanical hassles, and lowers the probability of having an accident.

Double, double, toil and trouble;
Fire burn and cauldron bubble . . .
For a charm of powerful trouble
Like a hell-broth boil and bubble.

Macbeth, Shakespeare

Cooking Techniques

Although one may be perfectly comfortable cooking in a kitchen, many of us are pretty poor at cooking outdoors: stirring food in a pot balanced precariously between two rocks over an open fire, having the inability to regulate the flame well, and having things either take forever to cook or burn and stick. Admittedly, a lot of this is a matter of getting used to one's equipment and experimenting with fires, but there are some techniques that make the transition from kitchen to outdoor cooking easier.

Meals cooked outdoors tend to burn easily because lightweight aluminum pans don't distribute heat well and backpack stoves concentrate flames in a limited area. To avoid burning foods cooked in a frying pan on a stove, use a lid and move the pan on the stove's burner to ensure even heating. Foods cooked in deep, large pots either with a stove or a fire need to be stirred constantly. Thickeners or ingredients like milk and cheese are best added at the last minute to foods being cooked. Dry solid starches like macaroni ought to be washed first and put only in boiling water so a soggy goop won't settle to the bottom of the pot.

Foods cooked at high altitudes dry out rapidly, too. A lid prevents such water loss but sometimes it is necessary to add extra water while cooking. One must sometimes be careful when adding spices to food—no two people have similar tastes, and spices once combined cannot be removed. Caution also is in order whenever rehydrating powdered mixes, for most manufacturers overestimate the amounts of water needed to be mixed to their dry products, resulting in thin soups or runny sauces. Noodles, macaroni, or non-instant rice have only to be cooked in enough water to rehydrate the dry starches completely. Such a procedure saves fuel by not heating up extra water that later will be dumped out. The starch taste is unnoticeable.

Powdered mixes can be reconstituted by adding small amounts of cold water to the mix itself, stirring to form a paste, then adding the remaining water. A similar procedure is employed for making up powdered milk, except a wide-mouth polybottle is used for a container. After stirring in the milk powder to remove lumps, The polybottle is shaken to completely dissolve all milk crystals, and the remainder of the water is added. Instant puddings are best mixed in a partially milk-filled polybottle, shaken vigorously for three minutes, then transferred immediately to a pot before setting takes place.

Traditionally, water used for cooking taken from high mountain lakes, streams, springs, or seeps was generally pure. Nowadays, studies have indicated that some streams in more popular mountain areas are no longer safe to drink without treatment. When water cleanliness is ever in question, the water ought to be purified. A water disinfectant must be able to kill the hardiest organisms, especially amoebic cysts and the viruses like infectious hepatitis. No method currently available to backpackers will purify their water 100 percent of the time. However, the techniques listed below will produce water free of pathogenic organisms almost always. These techniques are what most outdoor education schools use for treating their water.

The method used to purify water without chemicals is to boil it. This can be done by having water at a full boil for five minutes, letting the water sit for ten minutes, then bringing the water back to a boil for another five minutes. This double boil is equivalent to a noninterrupted twenty-minute boil.

Iodination is the other dependable technique which can kill organisms; there are three such iodination methods. One commonly used technique is adding 2-3 drops of two-percent tincture of iodine per quart of water. Such water has an unpleasand taste but is palatable. Another method is employing commercially manufactured Globaline tablets, widely distributed under the brand name Potable Aqua. One tablet per quart of untreated water ensures the proper concentration of iodine. Globaline tablets, though, are expensive and lose 20 percent of their effectiveness in six months. The other technique of iodination is the most complicated, but it is best suited for outdoor travelers after they have become familiar with the process. This method involves using a concentrated solution made from pure iodine crystals to treat questionable water. See Appendix IV for details. Halazone or bleach is not recommended for treatment of questionable water for both are ineffective against amoebic cysts or enteroviruses. In the near future, manufacturers will be marketing light weight water purifying units employing chemicals in conjunction with a microscreen filter.

To obtain actual amounts of water in winter, snow or ice can be melted in a pot. A small amount of water added to the pot keeps the pot's bottom from burning (which would produce an awful taste). A lid should be used on a pot whenever melting snow or ice over a wood fire. The lid prevents the smell of drifting smoke or falling ashes from contaminating the water.

Fires

Cooking with a fire is a time-consuming process because one has to gather wood, make the fire, continually tend to it and, finally, alleviate all its traces. Again, never build a fire in an area that ecologically or esthetically shouldn't have one. When having a fire, though, one ultimately wants a small fire with a hot bed of coals. In constructing the fire, care needs to be taken so that the fire site will contain the fire and not allow it to spread. To make such a site, dig a hole until non-organic soil is reached (four to six inches deep). Make the hole wide enough so the fire will not touch the hole's sides. When the organic ground cover extends further than a foot below the surface, a small fire can be built on a bed of rocks above the ground. Partially or fully surrounding the fire with rocks becomes necessary at times when it is windy. Any rocks used for a fire ought to be from areas other than stream beds (round rocks) or of slate origin, for these rocks contain moisture and will explode when heated.

To broil food on a campfire, suspend a pot over the fire with either a lashed tepee or rail arrangement from dead branches (see Figure 1). Pots may even be placed directly on small burning logs or coals themselves. If logs are employed as pot supports, new logs may be rolled beneath the pot as old pieces of wood burn up. Small lightweight metal grills can be used too. It is thus unnecessary to blacken rocks by using them as a pot support.

Figure 1:

Frying over a fire involves a little more fire construction technique on one's part than boiling. A hot bed of long-lasting coals is what is needed. Fairly large pieces of wood have to be burned to produce such coals (four inches in diameter is adequate). The harder the wood burned (oak or firs rather than cedar and aspen), the longer one's coals will last. Actual frying is done over a leveled coal bed moved slightly away from the fire's flames.

Baking foods like breads is the ultimate expression of one's cooking abilities. The secret of success in baking is keeping the food from getting too hot while cooking. If any part of a bread's batter is over 350 °F for a period of time, burning will result. Pans used to bake in need to be well oiled beforehand with margarine, vegetable oil, or grease. Foods are completely cooked when a pine needle or other thin stick inserted comes out completely clean.

There are many methods for baking foods. The most common way is with a "Dutch oven"—completely surrounding a pot with coals (see Figure 2).

Figure 2:

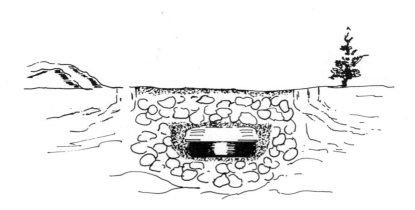

A Dutch oven is made by digging a shallow pit about half a foot deep and lining the bottom and sides with a heavy layer of hot coals. A thin covering of dirt or sand is placed on top of the coals to insulate the baking pot from the coals' direct heat. Place the pot with the food to be baked on this cool dirt layer and pack dirt completely around the pot's sides. A mound of coals is then placed on the pot's lid. Breads take approximately 20 to 25 minutes to cook by this method.

The following points need to be kept in mind when baking with a Dutch oven:

1. Best results are obtained by baking breads in shallow, narrow loaves. When any part of a bread's dough is more than several inches away from the pot's sides (like a two-quart pot half-filled with batter), the bread's center probably won't be cooked without burning its sides or bottom.

2. Coals on the pot's lid need to be periodically replaced with hot ones as they grow cold.

3. Let a bread bake at least fifteen minutes before inspecting to see if it is done unless, of course, one smells it burning. Checking too soon sometimes causes breads to "fall."

Another method of baking foods with a fire is to create a dry oven from two pots (see Figure 3). A dry oven is best used when one is baking lots of small cakes. Cooking time is approximately ten to fifteen minutes. The pot or cup holding the batter ought to be supported by as little surface as possible (a few pointed rocks) and not come in contact with the outside pot. The whole pot arrangement is placed on a bed of hot coals with some coals extending part way up the pot's sides. When baking with larger pots it is necessary to put coals on the pot's lid to ensure complete baking, especially when one is cooking thick breads. If the coals used are too hot, or when one cannot keep his hand close to the coals for several seconds, a hole is easily burned in the outside pot's bottom.

Foods may also be baked in a double boiler. The batter is placed in a small pot with a tight-fitting lid. That pot is then placed in a larger pot partially filled with water. Baking breads with a double boiler takes longer because the inside temperature of the pot never rises above 212 °F.

A simpler way to bake over a fire is to wrap some stiff batter around the end of a stick and cook directly over the coals. It is even possible to cook breads by a combination of frying pan and reflected heat (see Bannoc recipe). Reflector ovens also

Figure 3:

work well but few backpackers carry them because of their weight (2¾ pounds) and the need for large, blazing fires. Baking breads from heat reflected off surrounding propped-up rocks is extremely inefficient and not recommended.

Stoves

Cooking outdoors with a lightweight stove is almost the same as cooking at home except that there is only one burner. This is not as inconvenient as it appears if one cooks only one-pot meals. When several individual types of food are to be prepared, it is necessary to eat one course while another is cooking. For such a situation, stacking pot sets (see chapter on Cookware) are handy because food or a special sauce may be kept warm while something else is being heated over the stove. For other types of pots, like kettles, lids may be inverted upside down, filled with a sauce or cooked food, and fitted over the pot in order to keep the cooked food warm while something else is cooking. A small backpacking stove for four individuals is about the upper limit when cooking with a backpack stove.

Beyond that, incredibly large pots are necessary and cooking time becomes ridiculously long. For larger groups or more involved cooking, extra stoves or a stove-fire combination is recommended.

Baking over a stove is suggested only when one cannot bake with a fire, because baking takes an extremely long time and uses up lots of fuel. A typical bread needs 30 to 45 minutes to cook and even then may not be done. To bake with a stove, use the same double boiler dry oven arrangement as with a fire. For best results when baking over a stove, use small quantities of food—no more than a cup of batter per individual baked food. For those desiring to be especially fancy, Optimus manufactures a special oven for use with a backpacking stove, working on the same principle as a dry oven.

Cleaning up after oneself is a very important part of cooking technique, for there is an ever-increasing population of outdoor users, and the wilderness is shrinking. Lots of methods are available for washing cooking utensils and disposing of garbage. Glass, metal, and most plastic containers do not burn. If one carries them in, one can carry them out. Meals ought to be planned to minimize waste. Food weighs a lot and costs money; so why waste it by cooking too much food or sloppily preparing it? If soap is used in washing, the soap should be biodegradable, utilized in tiny amounts, and deposited far away from all possible water sources, preferably in a vegetated area. Fires are always messy. It is best to check with National Park or U.S. Forestry officials regarding their fire cleanup policies before going on a trip. With any method used in cleaning up after oneself, it ought to be the kind that will leave the least biological and visible impact on an area.

> *"Hey, Charlie, you're dumping soap in the river."*
> *"Ah, man, it's okay. This soap is biodegradable*
> *—it's natural. It's good for the fish and plants."*
>
> —Summer, '75, Outward Bound

"I made these Sierra trips, carrying only a sackful of bread with a little tea and sugar, and was thus independent and free ..."

—John Muir

Foods Commercially Available

There are many foods available from the supermarket which one can eat while backpacking. Specific recipes, like those comprising the bulk of this book, are not the only way to formulate one's outdoor menu. For instance, some store-bought cereals are ideal for a backpacker's breakfast. Outdoor lunches can be peanut butter and crackers, while a dinner is an instant sauce, cheese, and noodles. Listed are a group of foods that are commercially available and readily adaptable to the backpacker's needs—foods that are easy to carry, easy to use and prepare, good tasting, and nutritious. Suggestions are given too as to ways foods can be eaten for breakfasts and lunches. A sizeable number of different dinner combinations and ideas is presented to illustrate the idea of how evening meals are made.

One will find in actual shopping that the most economical way to purchase foods is at a large discount grocery store. Such a store not only is less expensive than a small neighborhood market but also has a greater variety of foods from which to choose. Whenever possible, it is best to buy foods in large quantities, too: twenty quarts of bulk powdered milk, for instance, instead of a six individual–quart package. There are a few foods, though, like whole wheat noodles, bulgar, cracked wheat, and sesame and sunflower seeds, that some supermarkets might not stock; or if they do, are prohibitively expensive. If such is the case, one can purchase these foods at a community granary or a local cooperative health food store.

Dairy Products and Oils

Powdered milk is a good food for backpackers because it is light in weight and high in protein. Powdered milk can be used to make sauces or puddings, can be added to drinks, consumed straight, or poured over cereals. Non-instant powdered milk is cheaper, slightly more concentrated, but is more troublesome to prepare than the instant types. On the trail, instant milk is superior because of its ease of preparation.

Cheese, like milk, is a very versatile backpacking food. Cheese is good for lunch and makes excellent dinner sauces. Dry and smoked varieties like Romano, Parmesan, and smoked Cheddar keep the best for they won't melt when it is hot outside and will keep for over a month without spoiling. Hard Cheddar and Swiss cheese are the next best to take on a trip for they become oily in hot weather and will spoil in several weeks if not eaten. Soft cheese like Gouda, Mozzarella, and Monterey Jack are not recommended for they are extremely greasy in hot summer conditions.

Instant eggs and omelettes are available in package form at a local supermarket. Powdered eggs are expensive but add variety to breakfasts. Eggs may also be combined with instant hash browns and rehydrated vegetable flakes to form omelettes or added to noodle-rice–type dinners to create a light, textured meal. Frequently, an inexpensive location to purchase powdered eggs is through your local bakery.

Butter can be taken on short backpack trips but will go rancid within a week in very hot weather. Margarine (preferably oleomargarine) is a better source of fat than butter for most margarines can be carried unrefrigerated for over several weeks without going rancid, and they do not burn easily. Margarine which has been repeatedly melted and solidified in its storage container still is good, though its appearance and taste have been slightly altered. Vegetable oils are another source of fat and are best used for frying. Liquid oil has a slightly higher caloric value than either margarine or butter.

Fruits, Vegetables, and Legumes

Fruits, dates, raisins, dried apples, peaches, apricots, and pears add variety to a backpacker's menu but weigh an appreciable amount for the caloric value they contain (see Appendix I). Cooking fruit in a meal rather than adding the fruit to food when it is done is the best way to get the most of the fruit's flavor and sweetness in a meal. Potatoes come in a variety of forms, the cheapest being dehydrated potato buds. Potato buds are useful not only for dinners but, when cooked and combined with flour and spices, become tasty potato pancakes. Other types of dry potato products include dehydrated hash browns and scalloped potatoes.

Lentils are also good sources of nutrition for the outdoor traveler, provided weight and time are not important factors. Legumes, like peas and beans, take too long to soften to enable one to use under most backpacking circumstances. Lentils are prepared by first grinding them at home in a blender. In the field, the lentils are then boiled in water for five minutes, and left to soak in the hot water for an hour before simmering them again for dinner. Minced onions, dehydrated vegetables, celery, and sweet green bell pepper flakes make excellent additions for most dinners that contain lentils. Vegetable seasonings can be purchased frequently in large bottles rather than in expensive small spice containers. Grated lemon and orange peel is available too and are good tasting in rice dinners.

Grains and Flour Products

Starches like rice and noodles form the basis of most backpacker's dinners. Rice comes in different types: precooked, white and brown rice, and in short and long grains. Precooked instant rice is fastest to prepare (five minutes sitting in water that has just boiled), but can only expand in the proportion of one to one with water. Regular rice takes longer to cook (15 minutes), but expands one to three with water and has a heavier-bodied texture. Regular brown rice takes 45 minutes of cooking time. Differences between short and long grain rice are mostly of personal tastes, the long type being crunchier. Bulgar and cracked wheat may also be used for dinners and breakfasts. Cracked wheat expands with water in a one to three proportion while bulgar expands one to two.

Macaroni, egg noodles, and spaghetti are frequently used for dinners too. Whole wheat macaroni is preferable to regular macaroni because it is higher in protein.

Cornmeal, and whole wheat and white flours can be used as a food source by backpackers. Cornmeal is good as a hot cereal, while flour is used for tortillas and thickening agents. Wheat germ can be used as an ingredient to supplement cereals. Self-rising flour mixes such as Bisquick offer advantages for people who like to prepare their own pancakes, biscuits, dumplings, and compotes, while not wishing to make their flour mixtures themselves. Store-bought corn or flour tortillas are convenient for enchiladas, quesadillas, and other Mexican meals. Corn tortillas are preferable to the flour type, lasting two to three weeks instead of the usual four to five days for the flour type.

Meats and Meat Substitutes

Any form of fresh meat, whether a cooked roast or raw hamburger, can be safely brought along on an overnight trip, or if one is traveling outdoors in winter when it is cold. For trips of up to a week in summer, when weight is not too crucial, meat may be brought in cans. Canned means available at a store include vienna sausage, liverwurst, deviled ham, chicken, corned beef, Spam, sardines in assorted sauces, albacore, tuna fish, and shrimp. For those desiring meat without metal containers, a semi-dried beef is sold by Armour that will last up to a week unrefrigerated once removed from its jar. Wilson Company sells "Bits O Bacon," real bacon bits with most of the fat removed. Bits O Bacon is almost identical in composition to the Wilson "Bacon Bars" which camping stores sell, but costs only a third as much. Bits O Bacon will last several weeks once the can is opened. Dry salami by Gallo keeps up to several years without refrigeration.

Substitutions for meat products are also available that are high in protein. Bac-O-Bits is texturized soy protein that tastes and looks somewhat like authentic bacon. Similar products such as GranBurger and Vita Burger are made to taste and look like hamburger. Such soy hamburger is best used in sauces for dinners like spaghetti. The protein value of nuts and seeds is high and, when complemented, frequently exceed the available protein of meat (see protein discussion in chapter on nutrition). Good nuts that are high in protein are peanuts and soya nuts, along with sunflower and sesame seeds. Sesame and sunflower seeds can be cooked directly into many of the rice and other grain-containing dinners.

Seasonings

Spices and other flavorings are an important addition to the backpacker's repertoire of food, for frequently a little bit of a certain spice or herb is all that is necessary to make an okay meal into an excellent meal. Listed below are some recommended flavoring agents to have along on a trip. The longer the outing and the more people along, the greater the number I bring.

Standard: Salt
Pepper
Sugar
Honey
Cinnamon
Onion powder
Garlic powder (or clove)
Mushrooms (dehydrated)
Vegetable flakes, parsley flakes, bell pepper flakes, celery flakes.

Extras and Specials:
Curry
Cumin or chili powder
Miso (soy curd)
Dried mustard
Paprika
Italian spice—oregano, rosemary, thyme, basil
Sweet spice—nutmeg, ginger, allspice, cardamon
Vanilla bean

Soups and Sauces

Endless varieties of one-pot dinners can be made by using commercially prepared soups and sauces. Most outdoor dinners consist of a starch base, a flavoring agent and/or thickener, and extras like meat or vegetables. Such soups and sauces are excellent for individuals not wishing to trouble themselves with spices nor desiring to make their own sauce combinations. Knorr and Maggi make equally good soups. Lipton also has good soups and are less expensive than Knorr's and Maggi's, but one has less of a variety to choose from. Bouillon cubes can also be employed as a flavoring agent. There is even a greater selection of sauces than soups on the market. Some brand names include Lawry's, Durkee's, and French's. Sauces come in two varieties—thick and thin. The words, sauce mix like hollandaise or cheese sauce mix delineate a mix that can be used to thicken dinners, while the word mix such as sloppy joe or sweet and sour mix are ingredients added mainly for flavoring.

At right are two tables listing soup and sauce combinations for one-pot meals. These tables are offered as models to get ideas of how one-pot meals can be made. There are some words of caution, though, in making up your own dinner combinations. First, check to see that one has all the ingredients to make up a sauce. A spaghetti sauce requires canned tomato sauce or paste. Consequently, the backpacker needs to bring dried tomato soup to make a good spaghetti sauce. Similarly, cheese and other sauces require milk, so having a store of powdered milk is necessary. Most sauce seasoning mixes like an enchilada sauce mix are extremely strong; it is therefore advised to try a little mix at a time, then taste it, instead of adding the whole seasoning package to your dinner. Soups are thinner than sauces; so when using a soup, drain all extra water from the starch base. Of course, in all one-pot meals a good source of fat and protein ought to be included too.

Table 1: One-Pot Dinner Suggestions—Sauces and Mixes

Base	Sauce	Seasonings	Extras
Rice	Cheese Sauce Mix		Dried beef
	Sweet and Sour Mix	Vegetable flakes	Mushrooms
	Spanish Rice Mix	Sweet bell pepper	Dried beef
	White Sauce Mix	Beef bouillon cubes	Dried beef
Noodles	Beef Stew Seasoning	Vegetable flakes	Dried beef
	Stroganoff & Sour Cream Sauce		Dried beef
	Tuna Fish Sauce		Albacore-tuna
	Spaghetti Sauce	Parmesan cheese	Salami-soy burger
Potato Buds	Gravy Mix	Onion flakes	Meat
Beans-Lentils	Chili Seasoning	Cheese	
	Sloppy Joe Mix, Tomato Soup	"	
	Enchilada Sauce, Tomato Soup	"	
Tortillas		Cheese, cumin	
	Enchilada Sauce	Cheese	Soy burger

Table 2: One-Pot Dinner Suggestions—Soups

Base	Soup	Seasonings	Extras
Rice	Tomato Soup	Vegetable & onion flakes Oregano	Meat
	Mushroom Soup	Cheese, onion powder	Mushrooms
	Oxtail Soup	Vegetable flakes	Fish, dried beef
Potato Buds—Noodles	Mushroom Soup Vegetable Beef Soup	Bac-O-Bits, onion flakes	Dried beef
Dumplings	Chicken Noodle Soup		Meat
Zweiback	Green Pea Soup	Baco-O-Bits, onion flakes	

37

Packaged Dinners

For those further desiring to limit the amount of time and preparation spent on getting all the ingredients for a dinner together, there are "semi-complete" dinners sold at the supermarket which usually require the addition of meat or another protein source. Everyone has used Kraft macaroni and cheese meals. Betty Crocker makes Noodles Stroganoff, Almondine, and Romanoff, while Rice-a-Roni markets beef flavor, Spanish, chicken, and fried rice mixes. There are other semi-complete dinners on the market such as Hamburger Helper. A package of fondue mix with crackers is a good dinner too.

Cereals

A great number of cereals sold at a supermarket can be taken backpacking. Commercially made Familla and Muesli, though expensive, are good instant cereals, requiring only milk to thicken. If one does not mind the added weight and bulk too much, one can bring any of the different types of granolas sold at the market. Cooked cereals such as oatmeal, Ralston, Wheatena, Malt O Meal, and others are good for breakfasts too. In winter, because of weight restrictions, it is preferable to choose cooked cereals that expand the most in hot water (Wheatena mixed one to four with water), and carry margarine to provide the extra calories. For real persnickety eaters, individual servings of instant packaged flavored oatmeal are available, too.

Breads and Crackers

Breads and crackers are usually the basis of most lunches, needing only spreads or filling to be complete. Breads are nice to have outdoors but dry out rapidly and usually get squished in one's pack, unless they are dense like rye or pumpernickel. Eating a few crackers with lots of margarine and peanut butter is a more economical weight-saving technique than eating bread to get needed calories. Crackers also don't spoil and take up less room. I prefer the kind of crackers that are big and wide so I can put a lot of filling or spread on them. Varieties of crackers that are good to take outdoors are Triskets, Rye Crisp, Zweiback, Melba Toast, varieties of milk biscuits, and graham crackers.

Candies and Desserts

Sweets are everyone's favorite and are always brought along. For candy, block semi-sweet cooking chocolate, M & M's, and plain old chocolate bars are good, though they do melt when it is hot outside. For folks desiring to take chocolate but are unable to pay the price, sweet carob bits are a good substitution. Toffee-type bars and hard candies are better if it is hot outside, while pastries like Pop Tarts and cookies are good for munching. For desserts, one can make jello or have one of the many varieties of instant puddings or cream gel desserts, along with instant whipped cream. If one wishes to be more elaborate and does not mind the chemicals, instant cheese cake is available or one may bake a regular commercial cake mix like Snack-n-Cake, date bars, gingerbread, or muffin mixes.

Beverages

It is pleasant to have a good beverage besides water to drink with any meal. I prefer tea, carrying it in bulk with a tea ball on long trips to save weight. Other drinks include instant coffee, Wylers, Tang, hot, diluted Jell-o, presweetened Kool-Aid, Instant Breakfast, or even bouillon. Plain instant hot chocolate like Swiss Miss is good for an early morning drink. It is recommended to add instant coffee, milk, vanilla, cinnamon, or nutmeg to a plain instant chocolate mix rather than buying the cafe au lait–type drinks that are prohibitively expensive and contains lots of extra chemicals.

"People usually fail when they are on the verge of success so give as much care to the end, as the beginning."

—Lao Tzu

Recipes

I have divided the recipes of this book into the areas of Breads, Bars and Candies, Meats, Dinners, Sauces and Thickeners, Cereals, Spreads, Desserts, and Beverages. This division is to categorize recipes and is not meant to be an itemized menu to plan trips by. Most of the recipes for breads, bars and candies, meats, and some cereals are intended to be prepared ahead of time, at home; the finished product is to be brought on the trip. Such recipes are designated with the words "home directions." With other recipes, like dinners, the ingredients are to be taken along and the food created while cooking outdoors. These recipes are designated by the words "trail directions." One will discover that the majority of the recipes presented will be novel to people, for I have purposely avoided recipes of common knowledge like how to cook hot cereal or prepare jello and instant pudding. The actual calories, amounts of Useable Protein, and finished food weight of each recipe included in the book are listed in Appendix III.

The quantities of all the dinner and some breakfast recipes have been designed for two people in mind and liberal amounts of food are proportioned. Other recipes like those for bars and candies make a given amount of food which is indicated by the recipe food weight. For those desiring to change quantities of a recipe, change quantities of ingredients in proportion to each other. The exception is when one desires to add more or less meat to a recipe. Changing meat proportions does not interfere with other protein ingredients in the recipes. The ingredients in all the recipes containing vegetable protein have been complemented to ensure receiving the greatest amount of Useable Protein. To satisfy individual tastes and create greater variety, though, spices, herbs, dried fruit, honey, sugar, other seasonings, and oil may be altered without affecting the protein value of the recipes.

Different pan shapes can be used in baking breads. I personally prefer to make several small loaves from one bread recipe. Small loaves fall apart less easily, carry better in a pack, and distribution of food weight can be more equally divided. I store most of my breads, bars, candies, and cereals in plastic bags. The ingredients for dinners and breakfasts, which are intended to be created on the trail, may also be carried in plastic bags, bagged as individual meals. Or, depending on the type and length of trip, individual bulk ingredients can be carried in separate plastic bags and mixed according to one's needs.

Unless otherwise stated, the following types of ingredients are used in recipes. Eggs, when needed, are AA large size. Polyunsaturated oils and margarine along with natural oil peanut butter is the type used in cooking and baking. White flour, when needed, is of the unbleached type, soy flour is full-fat, and powdered milk is instant. Unsweetened coconut is preferred along with untoasted wheat germ. It is preferable to use real extracts for flavorings rather than artificial ones. Any type of brown or white sugar or honey suffices. Sunflower seeds used are of the unsalted type, and it makes no difference if sesame seeds are hulled or not. Sesame and sunflower meal is nothing more than the seeds ground to a fine mixture. Rice called for in dinner recipes is regular white rice. Instant rice may be substituted for regular rice by decreasing the amount of water proportionally—one cup of instant rice needs one cup of water, while one cup of regular rice requires between two and two and a half cups of water to be cooked. Soups specified are the type contained all in one envelope like Knorr and Maggi varieties. If natural greens are used in making a salad, one ought to be experienced in identifying the local plants.

42

It is hoped that the recipes presented here will be used as a jumping-off point in creating your own recipes. A good rule for creating new foods is experiment—go ahead and try something new! Make foods which you enjoy while trying to maximize caloric value versus food weight, having protein amounts high, and reducing cooking time and preparation problems. I baked over 200 loaves of bread just to create some of the bread recipes within.

In all experimentation, I make careful notes of exactly what I did. Keeping track of what works and what does not allows me to predict with more certainty what the end product shall be when different foods in varying quantities are combined. Such information assists me in the future when I want to create a new food but don't know exactly how. I keep notes too of what meals I especially enjoy or despise. Reviewing such notes prior to a trip aids me in planning my new trip menu.

Breads

Portuguese Honey Bread

1 c.	margarine
½ c.	packed brown sugar
⅓ c.	light molasses
2 Tb.	honey
1 Tb.	sherry
½ c.	cold mashed potato (cooked & skinned)
1¼ c.	sunflower seeds
2¾ c.	whole wheat flour
½ c. + 1 Tb. soy flour, sifted
½ c. + 1 Tb. sesame meal (ground up sesame seeds)
⅔ c.	instant powdered milk
1 tsp.	anise seed
1½ tsp.	cinnamon
¼ tsp.	baking soda
	pinch of black pepper
½ c.	candied glazed fruit

Home directions: Cream margarine and sugar together well in a large bowl. Add molasses, honey, sherry, mashed potato and sunflower seeds, stirring in individually. In a separate bowl, combine flours, sesame meal, powdered milk, anise seed, cinnamon, baking soda, and pepper. Add candied fruit to dry ingredients, separating each piece and coating it with the dry mixture. Fold dry ingredients into wet mixture a little at a time, stirring constantly. Batter ought to be moist when done mixing.

Mold dough with hands, place into two greased 9x5 inch pans. Bake 1½ hours at 200° or until done. Do not overbake. When done, wait for bread to cool for 15 minutes before removing from pans. Wait until bread is at room temperature before storing in plastic bags.

Portuguese honey bread will keep for over two months if stored in airtight bags. The bread actually softens with age. For those desiring spicier bread, increase anise and cinnamon measurements by 1 tsp. each.

Logan Bread

½ c.   margarine
¼ c.   packed brown sugar
⅓ c.   vegetable oil
½ c.   dark molasses
½ c.   honey
1¼ c.   sunflower seeds
3¼ c.   whole wheat flour, sifted
½ c.   soy flour, sifted
⅔ c.   sesame meal
⅓ c.   instant powdered milk
1½ tsp. salt
1½ tsp. baking powder

Home directions: Cream margarine and sugar together well. Add oil, molasses, honey, and sunflower seeds, stirring each in individually. In another bowl, combine sifted flours, sesame meal, powdered milk, salt, and baking powder. Fold into wet ingredients a little at a time. It is necessary to do the final mixing with one's hands. Batter ought to be stiff and gritty.

Pat dough into a greased 9x9-inch pan so the bread is one inch thick. In a 300° preheated oven, bake for 40 minutes. Let cool 15 minutes before removing from pan. Complete cooling. Cut bread into 3-inch squares, wrapping each section in plastic or aluminum foil.

Logan bread is becoming a popular item to take along on a long trip. This bread will keep for over two months. Some people like to eat the bread as a breakfast bar.

Cherry-Berry Tea Bread

⅔ c.	margarine
⅔ c.	packed brown sugar
2	eggs
½ c.	ripe mashed banana (1 large)
1½ c.	whole wheat flour, sifted
½ c.	soy flour
½ c.	old-fashioned rolled oats
¾ c. + 2 Tb.	Virginia peanuts (measure, then chop)
2 tsp.	baking powder
½ tsp.	salt
¼ c.	instant powdered milk
¼ c.	blueberries, drained
¼ c.	cherries, drained

Home directions: Mix together margarine and sugar. Stir in beaten eggs and mashed banana. In a separate bowl combine the flours, oats, chopped peanuts, baking powder, salt, and dry milk together; coat the berries and cherries with this mixture. Add the dry and wet ingredients together, mixing slowly.

Bake batter in a 350° preheated oven for 50 minutes in a 9x5 inch pan. Let cool for 15 minutes before removing from pan. Bread must be completely cold before storing.

Pain au Chocolat

1 c.	margarine
¾ c.	packed brown sugar
6	eggs
1 Tb.	lemon juice
6 Tb.	sunflower seeds
1½ c. + 2 Tb.	whole wheat flour, sifted
¼ c.	soy flour, sifted
3 Tb.	powdered milk
1 tsp.	baking powder
1 c.	glazed candied fruit
6 oz.	semi-sweet chocolate chips

Home directions: Cream margarine and sugar together well. Individually stir in beaten eggs, lemon juice, and sunflower seeds. In a separate bowl mix together sifted flours, powdered milk, and baking powder. Add glazed fruit, coating each piece with dry ingredients. Slowly combine dry and wet mixtures, then stir in the chocolate chips.

Put batter into a greased 9x5 inch pan. Cook 40 minutes in a preheated 325° oven. Cool bread fifteen minutes before removing from pan. Let cool completely before storing in a plastic bag.

This bread will become one of your favorites. It will keep for over two months.

Pumpkin Bread

½ c.	vegetable oil
1 ¼ c.	packed brown sugar
2	eggs
¾ c.	canned pumpkin
¾ c. + 2 Tb.	sunflower seeds
1 c.	whole wheat flour, sifted
¾ c.	soy flour, sifted
½ tsp.	cinnamon
⅓ tsp.	salt
¼ tsp.	ginger
	pinch of clove
2 tsp.	baking powder
¾ c.	Virginia peanuts (measure, then chop)

Home directions: Combine oil and sugar. Individually stir in beaten eggs, pumpkin, and sunflower seeds. Mix together in another bowl the flours, cinnamon, salt, ginger, clove, and baking powder. Stir dry and wet ingredients together. Add chopped nuts.

Pour batter into a 9x5 inch pan. Cook for 25 minutes in a 325° preheated oven. Cool for 15 minutes before removing from pan. Let bread cool completely, then store.

Pumpkin bread lasts one week.

Golden Carrot Cake

1½ c.	packed brown sugar
¾ c.	margarine
4	eggs
1½ c.	grated carrots (4 large)
1¼ c.	sunflower seeds
1½ c. + 2 Tb.	whole wheat flour, sifted
¼ c.	soy flour, sifted
⅓ c.	ground sesame meal
⅓ c.	instant powdered milk
1 tsp.	cinnamon
1 tsp.	mace
1 Tb.	baking powder
½ tsp.	salt

Home directions: Combine sugar and margarine, creaming well. Individually fold in beaten eggs, grated carrots, and sunflower seeds. Mix in a separate bowl the flours, sesame meal, powdered milk, cinnamon, mace, baking powder, and salt; stir into wet ingredients slowly.

Pour batter into two 2½x6 inch bread pans or one large one. Cook for 35 minutes in a 325° preheated oven. Cool bread for 15 minutes before removing from pan. Let bread reach room temperature before wrapping in bags.

Golden carrot cake lasts for three weeks before spoiling.

Banana Nut Bread

½ c.	margarine
1 c.	packed brown sugar
2	eggs
1½ c.	mashed ripe bananas (3 large)
1 c.	whole wheat flour, sifted
¼ c.	soy flour, sifted
⅓ c.	instant powdered milk
1 tsp.	baking soda
½ tsp.	salt
1 c. + 3 Tb.	Virginia peanuts

48

Home directions: Cream together margarine and sugar. Add in beaten eggs. Mash ripe bananas and fold into wet ingredients. In a separate bowl combine sifted flours, dry milk, baking soda, and salt. Mix dry and wet ingredients together. Chop peanuts and stir in.

Pour batter into two 2½x6 inch greased pans or one large one. Cook for 30 minutes in a 300° preheated oven. Cool for 15 minutes before removing from pans. Completely cool before wrapping in plastic bags.

Banana nut bread will keep up to one week.

Bannoc

¼ c.	brown sugar
2 c.	whole wheat flour
⅓ c.	instant powdered milk
1 Tb.	baking powder
¼ tsp.	salt
¼ c.	raisins
2 Tb.	margarine
½ c.	water

Trail directions: Add brown sugar, whole wheat flour, powdered milk, baking powder, salt, and raisins together. Melt margarine and add to dry ingredients along with water, mixing well. Mold dough into two balls and place on an oiled frying pan lid near a fire. Cover with a towel and let dough rise for 20 minutes. Flatten dough balls and fry slowly in a lightly oiled skillet with a lid, lightly browning bread on both sides. Bake bread in a Dutch oven (see chapter on cooking techniques) with hot coals for 10 to 15 minutes.

Bannoc can be cooked by panfrying exclusively. Merely form dough into a greater number of thinner pieces and fry as above.

Bannoc dough may also be used to make Fry Bread. Mold dough into four balls and knead for several minutes. Flatten balls into a pancake shape, one-fourth inch thick. Place in hot oil and deep-fat fry (see Hush Puppies recipe) until lightly browned.

Fresh Corn Bread

1 c.	cornmeal
⅓ c.	soy flour
½ c.	whole wheat flour
⅔ c.	instant powdered milk
1 Tb.	baking powder
1 tsp.	salt
3 Tb.	honey
1½ c.	water

This is a bread whose ingredients can be measured ahead of time and made while on the trail.

When at home: Combine in a plastic bag cornmeal, soy, and whole wheat flours, powdered milk, baking powder, and salt.

Trail Directions: Gradually add water and honey to the dry ingredients, stirring well. Pour corn meal into a well-oiled frying pan lid. Place lid inside a larger pot and bake in a dutch oven (see chapter on cooking techniques). Cooking time approximately 20 minutes with hot coals. Check to see if done by inserting a pine needle into bread. Bread is done when needle comes out clean.

H & D Pancakes

½ c.	unbleached white flour
1 c.	whole wheat flour
⅔ c.	wheat germ, untoasted
⅓ c.	instant powdered milk
2 tsp.	baking powder
3 Tb.	brown sugar
1 tsp.	salt
2 Tb.	oil

Trail directions: Combine flours, wheat germ, powdered milk, baking powder, sugar, and salt; mix well. Slowly add water and oil, stirring until batter is completely mixed. Batter ought to be thick, yet easy enough to pour.

Cook pancakes on a well-oiled skillet with low heat and a lid.

Makes 8 *big* cakes.

Cathy's Biscuits

1 c.	unbleached white flour
1 c.	whole wheat flour
⅔ c.	instant powdered milk
4 tsp.	baking powder
1 tsp.	salt
¼ c.	vegetable oil
1 c.	water

In outdoor cooking biscuits, dumplings, compotes, and some cakes are derived from the same recipe. Differences arise only from how one cooks them and in a subtle change of a few ingredients.

Trail directions: To form biscuits, mix flours, powdered milk, baking powder, and salt together. Stir in ½ c. water and oil. Slowly add remaining water until biscuit dough becomes slightly tacky. Do not add more water beyond this point.

Form dough into two-inch balls, flatten down slightly and cook both sides in a frying pan using low heat and a lid. Biscuits may also be cooked in a Dutch oven (see Corn Bread recipe) or cooked on a stick over a fire with stiffer dough.

Dumplings are made by Cathy's Biscuit Recipe except the dough is formed into one-inch balls, placed into a boiling liquid, and simmered for approximately five minutes, using a lid.

A compote is nothing more than a huge dumpling. Most compotes are made for desserts but occasionally for a dinner too. The secret for a successful compote is to make the batter exceedingly stiff (i.e., use less water than for biscuits). Batter ought to have the consistency of a whole-grain bread dough. Flatten dough out so it is about one-half inch thick and nearly the diameter of the pot it will be cooked in. The dessert or dinner in which the compote will be cooked ought to have the consistency of a thick stew and be almost completely cooked. Cook with lid on for about 5-7 minutes.

Bars and Candies

No-Bake Fudge

2 c.	chocolate chips
1 c.	butterscotch chips
¼ c.	honey
¼ c.	coconut
¼ c. + 2 Tb.	sunflower seeds
⅓ c.	sesame meal
⅓ c.	instant powdered milk
¼ c.	instant oatmeal
¼ c.	untoasted wheat germ
¼ c.	wheat bran

Home directions: Melt chocolate and butterscotch chips together in a double boiler; add honey. Combine coconut, sunflower seeds, sesame meal, dry milk, oatmeal, wheat germ, and bran together in a separate bowl. Stir dry ingredients with liquid, mixing well. Mold into a 9x9 inch pan. Let set overnight before cutting and wrapping in cellophane.

Breakfast Bars

2⅔ c.	old-fashioned oatmeal
½ c. + 1 Tb.	whole wheat flour
6 Tb.	soy flour
⅓ c.	instant powdered milk
6 Tb.	sesame seeds
½ c.	brown sugar
¼ tsp.	cinnamon
1½ tsp.	salt
½ c.	oil
¾ c.	honey
2 tsp.	vanilla extract

Home directions: In a bowl mix together oatmeal, whole wheat flour, soy flour, powdered milk, sesame seeds, brown sugar, cinnamon, and salt. Heat in a pan: oil, honey and vanilla extract; when mixed add to dry ingredients, stirring well.

Pat batter in a 9x13 inch pan; bars ought to be ½ inch thick. Place in a 325° preheated oven and cook for 30 minutes.

Coffee Toffee Bars

1 c.	margarine
1 c.	packed brown sugar
2	eggs
1 Tb.	pure almond extract
2 c. + 3 Tb.	whole wheat flour, sifted
⅔ c.	soya nuts
½ c.	sesame meal
3 Tb.	instant coffee
6 oz.	chocolate chips, semi-sweet (1 cup)
1 tsp.	baking powder
1½ tsp.	salt

Home directions: Cream together margarine and brown sugar. Add in beaten eggs and almond extract. In a separate bowl combine flour, nuts, sesame meal, coffee, chocolate chips, baking powder, and salt.

Mix dry and wet ingredients together. Pour into greased 9x9 inch pan and bake in a 350° preheated oven for 20-25 minutes. When done, let cool in pan for 15 minutes before removing. When cold, slice into squares and wrap.

Scotch Shortbread

1 c.	salted butter
½ c.	white sugar
1 tsp.	vanilla
2 c.	whole wheat flour, sifted
⅓ c.	soy flour, sifted
¼ c. + 2 Tb.	sesame meal

Home directions: Mix sugar and butter together for several minutes. Stir in vanilla. Combine already mixed flours and sesame meal to wet ingredients. Divide mixture into six parts. Form each part into a ball and knead each ball with hands for several minutes. Mold balls into patties ¾ inch thick and place on a cookie sheet.

Cook at 350° in a preheated oven for 18 minutes or until lightly golden. Do not overcook.

Flapjacks

½ c.   margarine
½ c.   brown sugar, packed
¼ c.   honey
¼ c.   dark corn syrup
¾ tsp.   mapeline (optional)
2½ c.   old-fashioned rolled oats
⅔ c.   soya nuts
¼ Tb.   sunflower seeds

Home directions: Cream margarine and sugar together. Individually stir in honey, syrup, and mapeline (optional). Chop soya nuts and mix with sunflower seeds and oatmeal; add to wet ingredients.

Pat mixture into a 9x13 inch pan, no thicker than a ½-inch layer. Place in a 350° preheated oven for 30-35 minutes. When done, set aside to cool. Cut in squares and wrap.

Flapjacks is an old Outward Bound and wilderness canoeist's favorite. The food is extremely dense and rich.

Ohm Balls

½ c.   honey
¼ c.   vegetable oil
½ c.   sunflower meal (finely ground up sunflower seeds)
½ c.   sunflower seeds
⅔ c.   sesame meal (finely ground up sesame seeds)
⅓ c.   instant powdered milk
½ c.   carob powder
½ c.   coconut

Home directions: Stir in honey and oil together in a deep bowl. Mix in sunflower seeds. Combine sunflower and sesame meals together with powdered milk, carob, and coconut, mixing well. Slowly add to wet ingredients.

Divide batter into eight parts; make into balls and knead with hands for several minutes. Wrap in cellophane.

Ohm Balls have become a favorite for many Alaskan expeditions. They are not overly sweet, yet provide lots of quick energy.

Peanut Brittle

1 c.	water
¾ c.	raw peanuts, unsalted
1 c.	raw sunflower seeds
1½ c.	white sugar
¾ c.	light corn syrup
1 tsp.	salt
2 Tb.	margarine
¼ tsp.	baking soda
	Candy thermometer

Home directions: Boil 1 c. water. Remove from heat and add peanuts, sunflower seeds, sugar, corn syrup, and salt. Bring to a slow boil again, stirring constantly to avoid burning. At 290° (or when a small amount of syrup when dropped into cold water will separate into threads, which will then be hard and brittle when removed from the water), stir in quickly melted margarine and baking soda. Pour peanut brittle onto two warmed Teflon cookie sheets, spreading so that candy is about ¼ inch thick.

Let peanut brittle sit until completely cool. Break up into small pieces and store.

Peanut brittle can be made while traveling outdoors, too.

Sesame Bombs

⅓ c.	instant powdered milk
½ c.	coconut
1½ c.	sesame meal
¼ c.	honey

Home directions: Combine powdered milk, coconut, and sesame meal together; add to honey, mixing well. Form dough into two-inch balls and knead with hands for several minutes. Flatten each ball out on cookie sheet, ½ inch thick. Bake in a 300° preheated oven for 20 minutes. Cool and package.

Sesame Bombs are a good-tasting, long-lasting candy. It packs extremely well and won't spoil over time.

Gunk

⅓ c.	instant powdered milk
¼ c.	carob powder
6 Tb.	sesame meal
½ c.	untoasted wheat germ
¾ c.	creamy peanut butter
¾ c.	honey
¼ c.	sunflower seeds
½ c.	coconut

Home directions: Combine dry milk, carob, sesame meal and wheat germ. Heat peanut butter and honey in saucepan until melted; stir in sunflower seeds. Remove from heat and quickly add to it the milk/carob/sesame/wheat germ mixture. Stir in coconut.

Form mixture into round balls or several bricks. Let cool completely before wrapping.

Gorp

¾ c.	peanuts
1 c.	sunflower seeds
¾ c.	raisins
1	8-oz. package semi-sweet chocolate chips or carob chips

Home directions: Mix peanuts, sunflower seeds, raisins, and chocolate chips together in a plastic bag.

Set bag out in the warm sun for several hours so chocolate gets soft and conceals the rest of the ingredients. (Carrying gorp in the outside pocket of one's pack accomplishes the same thing.) Place gorp deep inside of a pack to avoid re-melting.

Everyone has their own tastes for gorp. This recipe is high in protein and maximizes calories versus food weight. For those desiring a gorp of individual pieces, use chocolate M& M's instead of chocolate chips.

Marzipan

1	egg white
1 c.	pure almond paste
1½ c.	sifted confectioner's sugar
½ c.	grated coconut

Home directions: Whip egg white and mix in almond paste, mashing with a fork. Slowly stir in confectioner's sugar, a little at a time, then coconut. If too much sugar is added and marzipan becomes hard, a few drops of lemon juice will soften it. Shape marzipan into small bars and wrap in cellophane or plastic bags.

Marzipan is a very sweet candy and will provide lots of quick energy. It is very easy to make, won't get runny when it is hot outside and keeps well for long periods of time.

Sesame Crunch

1 Tb.	non-salted butter
½ c.	light corn syrup
¼ c.	white granulated sugar
2 Tb.	instant powdered milk
½ c.	sesame meal
	Candy thermometer

Home directions: On low heat, melt butter, corn syrup, and sugar in a deep-sided, clean pot, stirring until mixed. Keep heat low and cook for 3 minutes with a tight-fitting lid on. Meanwhile, mix dry milk and sesame meal together in another bowl. Insert clean candy thermometer into heated pan and slowly bring up temperature to 280°F, then turn off heat and in the next 15 seconds stir in sesame/milk mixture, mix completely and pour onto a Teflon-surfaced frying pan. Mold mixture flat, ½ inch thick. Let sit until cool. Cut into desired amounts, then wrap.

For those desiring a stronger tasting candy, use ¼ c. dark corn syrup and ¼ c. light corn syrup in place of all light corn syrup.

This candy is extremely good and very addicting.

Apricot Leather

2 c.   water
2 c.   dried fruit (approximately 11 oz.)—apricots
         preferred but apples and peaches work too
2 Tb.   honey

Home directions: Place 2 c. of boiling water over dried fruit.
Let sit 24 hours and then drain.

Blend fruit in a blender with honey until fruit has a jam-like
consistency. Spread fruit very thin on two Teflon cookie sheets
and dry in an oven with only a pilot lamp lit for two days. Peel
off cookie sheet and roll up in saran wrap.

Note: Dried fruit is exceedingly expensive these days. An alternative to buying dried fruit is to dry your own fruit, especially
apples. For apples, peel and core them. Cut apples into thin
slices and hang slices on a string in a kitchen or other room
where they won't be disturbed for approximately two weeks.

Meats

Dried Beef

2 lbs.   lean meat (beef round, flank steak, etc.)
2 c.   water
½ c.   salt
½ Tb.   black pepper
¼ c.   vinegar

This recipe allows one to bring meat on a trip without having to worry about it spoiling. The dried beef may be rehydrated by adding the meat to boiling water for 5 minutes. Two pounds of lean meat produces approximately two-thirds of a pound of dried beef.

Home directions: Trim fat from meat. Slice meat into quarter-inch strips, slicing with the grain of the meat. Prepare a brine solution by combining the water, salt, pepper, and vinegar in a deep pot and bring to a boil. Divide sliced meat into four lots. Boil each lot in brine solution for five minutes (by the clock), keeping brine solution boiling the whole time. Meat will be grayish in color when done. Press out juices with rolling pin and paper towels. If red juice comes out of the pressed meat, the meat is not cooked enough.

Place individual strips of pressed meat on metal oven racks in a 150° preheated oven, keeping oven door slightly ajar. Meat will dry in 1½ hours. The meat ought to have a tendency to crack but should not be brittle. If meat bends but does not break, cook longer in oven. Store strips.

Dried beef will keep for a long time. Best to use before two months. Brine solution is enough for 2½ pounds of meat.

Tak's Beef Jerky

3 lbs.	lean beef, preferably flank steak
¼ c.	soy sauce
⅓ c.	Worcestershire sauce
¼ c.	sherry
1 tsp.	onion powder
1 Tb.	salt
½ tsp.	black pepper
	pinch of ginger

Home directions: Trim all fat from meat. Slice meat into ¼-inch strips, cutting with the meat's grain. Mix seasonings to form sauce. Combine meat and sauce in a plastic bag and marinate overnight in a refrigerator. Next day drain sauce and pat meat dry with paper towels. Place strips of meat on oven racks approximately 8 hours to dry, with only pilot light heat.

One pound of raw meat will make approximately one-third pound of jerky.

Beef jerky, when stored in a plastic, bag, will keep for several months.

Pemmican

2 lbs.	lean meat (beef round, flank steak, etc.)
2 c.	water
½ c.	salt
½ tsp.	black pepper
¼ c.	vinegar
2 lbs.	pure kidney fat (cow's)
⅓ c.	chopped raisins
⅓ c.	white granulated sugar

Home directions: To begin, prepare meat as in Dried Beef recipe, but slice meat *across* the grain. When meat is dried, place the meat in a blender for about 15 seconds to make it into fine bits.

Take the kidney fat and peel or slice off any dried beef juices or membranes. Break the fat into small pieces and melt in a pot over low heat, being careful never to let the fat boil. Strain the pot's contents through a metal strainer and retain the strained-out pure melted oil—this saved oil is suet and will be used.

Measure how much dried beef has been prepared. For every cup of dried beef there needs to be a proportional amount of 2 Tb. of sugar, 2 Tb. chopped raisins and ⅓ c. suet. Combine dried beef, raisins, and sugar. Heat up the required amount of suet and mix it with the sugar/raisin/beef mixture to form pemmican. Let the pemmican completely cool before storing in a sealed container. Two pounds of lean meat makes approximately 20 ounces of pemmican.

Pemmican is an ideal food for outdoor travelers for it is extremely high in calories and supplies protein. Most pemmican available today does not contain fat, an essential ingredient. To make a real pemmican that won't go rancid, use only pure kidney fat which is available at a meat market. Pemmican made with kidney fat will keep over a year. Chopped apricots may be substituted for raisins to increase variety.

Dinners

Tangy Rice

¼ c.	margarine
¼ c.	white flour
⅔ c.	instant powdered milk
6 c.	water
2 oz.	grated cheese (part Parmesan, Jack or Swiss)
1½ c.	white rice
½ tsp.	cinnamon
½ tsp.	ginger
1½ tsp.	salt

Trail directions: In a frying pan (or the lid of the rice pot), melt and bring to a boil the margarine. Add in flour and simmer for several minutes, stirring constantly. Mix two cups water to powdered milk. Pour milk slowly into sauce, stirring; simmer until it thickens. Add in grated cheese, stirring as little as possible.

In a separate pot, add salt, cinnamon, ginger, rice, and four cups of water. Bring to a boil and simmer. When rice is done, drain; serve with cheese sauce poured over.

Cheese sauce may be kept hot while rice is cooking by placing lid containing sauce on top of pot while rice is cooking.

Sea of Cortez

¾ c.	white rice
⅔ c.	bulgar
6 Tb.	soy grits
1½ tsp.	salt
2 Tb.	curry
4 c.	water
3 Tb.	honey
¼ c.	raisins (optional)
¼ c.	margarine

Trail directions: Combine in a pot rice, bulgar, soy grits, salt, and curry with four cups of water. Bring to a boil; add honey and raisins if desired. Simmer with lid for 15 minutes. Garnish with margarine and serve.

Rice and Milk

1½ c.   white rice
½ c.   raisins or other dried fruit
⅓ c.   sesame seeds
1½ tsp. salt
5½ c.   water
⅔ c.   instant powdered milk
1½ Tb.   cinnamon
2 Tb.   brown sugar (or to taste)
¼ c.   margarine

Trail directions: Bring rice, raisins, sesame seeds, and salt to a boil in 4 c. water. Simmer 15 minutes, covered. Mix powdered milk and 1½ c. water.

Serve rice with concentrated milk. Garnish with cinnamon, sugar, and margarine.

Note: Nutritionally it is preferable to use sesame meal (⅔ c.) instead of sesame seeds. Sesame seeds need to be chewed entirely to derive their full nutritive value.

Chicken-Rice Curry

1½ c.   white rice
¼ c.   raisins
4 Tb.   margarine
4 c.   water
1 pkg.   chicken noodle soup
2 Tb.   curry
1 small can of chicken

Train directions: Saute rice and raisins in margarine. Add 4 c. of water, chicken soup, and curry; bring to a boil, then simmer for 15 minutes. When almost cooked, stir in chicken.

Beef Stroganoff

4½ c.	water
⅔ c.	instant powdered milk
1 pkg.	sour cream mix
1 pkg.	stroganoff mix
2 c.	egg noodles (whole wheat noodles if possible)
½ c.	dried beef (see recipe)
2 tsp.	salt
4 Tb.	margarine

Trail directions: Mix 1½ c. of water with ½ c. powdered milk. In a pot add milk to sour cream and stroganoff mixes; heat and simmer until sauce thickens.

Place noodles, dried beef, salt, and 3 c. of water in a large pot. Bring to a boil and simmer for 15 minutes. Stir in combined stroganoff and sour cream sauce. Add margarine and serve.

Chicken Noodle Stew

3¾ c.	water
1½ c.	whole wheat noodles
1 pkg.	chicken noodle soup
¾ c.	unbleached white flour
¾ c.	whole wheat flour
⅓ c.	instant powdered milk
3 tsp.	baking powder
1 tsp.	parsley
1 tsp.	salt
3 Tb.	oil
1 small can of chicken	

Trail directions: Bring 3 c. of water to a boil. Add noodles and chicken noodle soup. Place lid on pot and simmer for 15 minutes.

In the meantime, mix flours, powdered milk, baking powder, parsley, and salt together. Stir in ¾ c. of water and oil. Batter will be stiff. Form batter into dumplings by making round balls one inch in diameter.

When noodles are almost done, simmer for 10 minutes; stir in chicken and add dumplings. Place lid on, lower heat, and simmer for 5-7 minutes until done.

Vegetable beef soup and dried beef (see recipe) may easily be substituted for chicken soup and canned chicken.

Chapades

1½ c.	whole wheat flour
½ c.	unbleached white flour
⅓ c.	instant powdered milk
¼ c.	sesame seeds
½ tsp.	salt
⅔ c.	water (approximate)
4 Tb.	margarine

Chapades is a traditional food for people living in the mountains of Nepal. This recipe is a variation from that food. Most people will be unaccustomed to such a plain tasting meal. Therefore, one might wish to add a pinch of onion powder to the batter. Or, when frying the second side of the chapade, add a layer of thinly sliced cheese and cover with a lid.

Trail directions: Mix flours, milk, sesame seeds, and salt together. Add enough water to mixture so dough may be formed into thin patties. In a lightly oiled pan, fry on low heat, browning both sides.

Chapade dough can also be deep-fat fried to make Fry Bread. Mold dough into palm-sized balls and knead for several minutes. Flatten balls into a pancake shape, one-fourth inch thick. Place in a skillet or pot containing oil (see Hush Puppies recipe) and cook until lightly browned.

A variation to Fry Bread is to add cheese to the inside of the dough, creating a torte. Form dough into very thin patties of tortilla thickness. Place thin strips of cheese and cumin on one side of dough. Fold dough over onto itself, pinching sides closed. Deep-fat fry as above. If dough does not stick together, wet dough edges with a few drops of water and pinch again. Be certain to roll the torte occasionally to ensure complete cooking.

Chipped Beef

2½ c.   water
1 c.   dried beef (see recipe)
4 Tb.   margarine
½ tsp.   salt
6 Tb.   unbleached white flour
⅓ c.   instant powdered milk
3 oz.   cheese—Cheddar, dry Jack, or Colby
1 small pkg. of Zwieback or hard bread

Trail directions: Place dried beef in 1 c. water. Bring to boil and simmer for five minutes. Drain water and save.

Melt margarine in a pot. Bring to a slow boil and slowly mix in salt and flour. Simmer 1 minute, stirring constantly. Mix dry milk with 1½ c. water; then add milk and salt to flour-margarine sauce, simmering until sauce thickens. Slice cheese into thin pieces and add to sauce along with rehydrated meat. Stir cheese into sauce as little as possible. Pour sauce over Zwieback.

One could also make Beef Cheddarton by pouring chipped beef sauce with a serving of cooked hash brown potatoes.

Tamale Pie

¾ c.   dried beef (see recipe)
⅓ c.   onion flakes
¼ c.   dried green pepper flakes
¼ c.   vegetable flakes
¼ c.   dried mushrooms
4 c.   water
2 pkg.   Lipton Cup-a-Soup, tomato
2 Tb.   chili powder
¼ tsp.   garlic powder
1 tsp.   salt
¼ tsp.   black pepper
4 Tb.   margarine
½ c.   cornmeal

Trail directions: Place dried beef, onion, green pepper and vegetable flakes, mushrooms, and 3½ c. water in a pot. Bring to a boil, remove from heat and let sit for 10 minutes. Stir in 2 packages tomato soup, chili and garlic powder, salt, pepper, and margarine. Bring to a boil. Combine corn meal with ½ c. water. Slowly stir corn meal paste into boiling vegetable-spice mixture. Simmer for 15 minutes. Serve when completely thickened.

Arroz Con Queso

1¼ c.	white rice
3 pkg.	Lipton Cup-a-Soup, tomato
1	garlic clove, chopped
¼ c.	dehydrated onion flakes
¼ c.	dehydrated sweet bell pepper
2 tsp.	dried basil
1 tsp.	oregano
1½ tsp.	salt
¼ c.	margarine
4 c.	water
1 c.	grated cheese

Trail directions: Combine rice, tomato soup, garlic clove, onion flakes, bell peppers, basil, oregano, margarine and salt in a pot with 4 c. of water. Bring to a boil and simmer covered for 20 minutes.

Place rice mixture on warmed tortillas. Cover lightly with cheese and serve.

You may also eat arroz con queso by putting the rice mixture and cheese on a tortilla, rolling it up, then frying the tortilla on both sides.

Oxtail Soup

1 package oxtail soup (Knorr, Maggi)
¼ c.   dehydrated vegetable flakes
5½ c.   water
1½ c.   white rice
1 c.   dried beef (see recipe)
½ tsp.   salt
4 Tb.   margarine

Trail directions: Place oxtail soup, vegetable flakes, and two cups of water in a frying pan lid. Bring to a boil and simmer until soup has thickened.

In a pot add rice, dried beef, salt, and 3½ c. of water. Bring to a boil, then simmer for 15 minutes. Stir in margarine and oxtail sauce.

Boiled fish and oxtail soup are also excellent. Part of a package of instant wine sauce is good in the meal too.

Macaroni and Cheese

4 Tb.   margarine
¼ c.   unbleached white flour
⅓ c.   instant powdered milk
4½ c.   water
4 oz.   cheese (2 oz. Cheddar or Parmesan,
              2 oz. Swiss of Jack), thinly sliced
1½ c.   whole wheat macaroni
1½ tsp. salt

Trail directions: In a pot melt margarine and bring to a boil. Mix in flour and simmer for about a minute, stirring constantly. Prepare milk by mixing powdered milk with 1½ c. water and combine to flour-margarine mixture. Simmer for several minutes until sauce thickens. Add cheese.

In a separate pot, combine noodles, salt, and 3¼ c. water. Bring to a boil and simmer with a lid for 15 minutes. Add cheese sauce and serve.

Cheese sauce may be kept warm by using pot lid to prepare the sauce and then using it as a cover while simmering the noodles in a pot below.

Chili Mac

½ c.	dried beef (see recipe)
1½ tsp.	salt
¼ tsp.	black pepper
2 Tb.	chili powder
3 c.	water
1½ c.	whole wheat noodles
⅓ c.	instant powdered milk
4 Tb.	margarine

Trail directions: Break dried beef into tiny ¼-inch pieces. Place dried beef, salt, pepper, chili powder, and 3 c. of water in a pot; bring to a boil. Add noodles and simmer with a lid for 15 minutes. When done, stir in powdered milk and margarine. Parmesan cheese topping is optional.

Lentils of Course

1 c.	dried, ground lentils
¼ c.	dehydrated minced onion
1½ Tb.	cumin or chili powder (preferably cumin)
2 tsp.	garlic powder
2 Tb.	honey or sugar
3 c.	water
1 tsp.	salt
4 Tb.	margarine
4 oz.	cheese (preferably Jack)

Trail directions: Place lentils, onion flakes, cumin, garlic powder, honey, water, and salt in a pot. Boil for two minutes. Cover pot and let lentils sit for one hour.

After one hour, bring to a boil again, add margarine, and simmer 15 minutes with lid. Garnish with thinly sliced cheese and serve.

Lentils are a good source of nutrition for the backpacker if one has the time to prepare them properly.

Rice Pilaff

1 c.	white rice
¼ c.	sunflower seeds (measure, then chop)
3 Tb.	dried parsley
4 Tb.	margarine
2½ c.	water
1 tsp.	salt
2½ Tb.	Parmesan cheese
⅓ c.	instant powdered milk

Trail directions: Saute rice and chopped sunflower seeds with parsley and margarine for five minutes. Add water and salt; bring to a boil, then simmer for 15 minutes. Stir in cheese and powdered milk. Serve.

There are many variations to this recipe. For instance, saute rice and sunflower seeds for five minutes. Add 2½ cups of chicken bouillon broth (2 bouillon cubes dissolved into 2½ c. of water), ⅓ c. dried celery flakes, and ¼ c. raisins. When rice is almost cooked, mix in ¼ c. non-instant powdered milk and serve.

Lentil Stew

¼ c.	dried, ground lentils (chopped in a blender)
1	bay leaf
2 Tb.	miso
½ c.	dried beef
⅓ c.	minced onion flakes
2	garlic cloves
1 tsp.	salt
¼ tsp.	black pepper
3½ c.	water
⅔ c.	white rice
¼ c.	vegetable oil

Trail directions: Combine lentils, bay leaf, miso, dried beef, onion flakes, garlic cloves (mashed), salt, pepper, and water in a large pot. Bring to a boil for two minutes. Turn off heat and let lentils sit covered for one hour.

After an hour, add rice and oil. Bring to a boil and simmer covered for 15 minutes.

Enchiladas

½ pkg. of enchilada sauce mix
4 pkg. Lipton Cup-a-Soup, tomato
¼ c. dehydrated sweet bell peppers
2 Tb. onion flakes
4 Tb. margarine
3 c. water
6 oz. cheese—Cheddar, Jack or Colby
6 flour or corn tortillas

Trail directions: Mix enchilada sauce, tomato soup, bell peppers, onion flakes, and margarine with 3 c. water in a pot. Bring to a boil and simmer for five minutes, stirring constantly.

Slice cheese and roll up in tortillas. Place tortillas in a large frying pan, covering with sauce. Any remaining cheese may then be added on top of sauce. Cover and simmer with low heat for 5-10 minutes until cheese begins to melt and sauce is very hot. Serve.

If such pot sets are available, a double boiler arrangement is preferable to a frying pan in heating up the enchiladas. Also, GranBurger or other soy texturized meat goes well with cheese inside the rolled up tortillas.

Quesadillas

4 Tb. margarine
6 corn tortillas
6 oz. cheese—Cheddar, Colby, Swiss
2-3 Tb. cumin

Trail directions: With low heat, melt some of the margarine in a frying pan. Lightly brown one side of a tortilla in the pan. Turn over, sprinkle sliced cheese and cumin on the other side, cover pan with lid and cook. When tortilla is completely fried and cheese has melted, serve.

French Onion Soup

1 pkg. French Onion Soup Mix
1 small pkg. of melba toast or
     seasoned Rye Crisp
6 oz. cheese—Cheddar, Colby, Jack, etc.

Trail directions: Prepare onion soup mix by adding half as much water as directed on package (about two cups). Break up crackers and place on the bottom of two bowls. Cover crackers with grated cheese. Pour hot soup on top of cheese. Serve.

French onion soup is a good dish. It is usually eaten in conjunction with something else to make a more filling dinner.

Cheese Blitz

1 pkg.	mushroom soup mix
2/3 c.	water
6 oz.	cheese—Swiss, Jack, or Cheddar
1 c.	whole wheat flour
1 c.	unbleached white flour
1/3 c.	instant powdered milk
1/2 tsp.	salt
4 Tb.	margarine
1 1/2 tsp.	paprika

Trail directions: Prepare mushroom soup mix, using half the amount of water recommended on the package. Slice cheese into thin pieces.

In a bowl, mix together milk, flour, and salt. Add ½ cup of water and stir. Dough ought to bind together. Add remaining water, a tablespoon at a time, until dough becomes tacky. Divide dough in half. Shape into two balls.

Flatten dough balls into two nine-inch diameter crusts. Fry in hot oiled skillet briefly on one side. Place cheese on half of fried crust and cook with lid until cheese melts. Fold in half, spoon over mushroom sauce and sprinkle paprika on top. Serve.

Spaghetti

6 c.   water
2 tsp.   salt
¼ lb.   spaghetti noodles
4 pkg.   Lipton Cup-a-Soup, tomato
½ pkg.   spaghetti sauce mix with mushrooms
¼ c.   oil
½ lb.   sliced salami
2 oz.   grated Parmesan cheese

Trail directions: Bring 4 c. of water to a boil in a large pot. Add salt. Add spaghetti noodles slowly to avoid breaking them. Turn heat low and simmer for 15 minutes. Meanwhile, in a separate pot, add 2 c. of water to combined spaghetti sauce, tomato soup, oil, and sliced salami. Bring sauce to a boil; simmer for 10 minutes.

Drain spaghetti noodles, pour sauce over them, sprinkle with cheese and serve.

Spaghetti sauce is ideally suited for using GranBurger or other texturized soy vegetable products. Merely mix the rehydrated soy meat in with the cooking spaghetti sauce.

Chinese Cuisine

½ c.   dehydrated onion flakes
4 c.   water
2 Tb.   miso
4 oz.   Chinese noodles
1   2-oz. can sardines packed in oil

Trail directions: Soak onion flakes in water for one hour; drain. In a pot, combine the onions and miso with four cups of water. Bring this mixture to a boil and stir until miso is completely dissolved. Add the noodles and diced sardines and continue boiling for three minutes. Stir while boiling to separate the noodles. Serve.

Skillet Pizza

½ tsp.	oregano
½ tsp.	rosemary
¼ tsp.	sage
¼ tsp.	basil
¼ tsp.	black pepper
½ tsp.	onion powder
4 pkg.	Lipton Cup-a-Soup, tomato
2 c.	water
4 oz.	salami
4 Tb.	margarine
	Seasoned Rye Crisp—4 large wafers
6 oz.	cheese—Jack or Swiss
2 oz.	Parmesan cheese

Trail directions: In a pot, combine spices with tomato soup. Add water, bring to a boil and simmer for 10 minutes with a lid.

Slice salami thin and fry it along with greased Rye Crisp (one wafer at a time) in a pan using low heat and a lid. After first side of Rye Crisp is done, turn over and add to it a thin layer of sauce. Sprinkle with cheese and add on fried salami. Place lid on pan and cook until done. Garnish with Parmesan cheese.

The key to success is using low heat and frying with lots of margarine. Skillet pizza, like the spaghetti recipe, is suited to using GranBurger or other texturized vegetable products. Rehydrate the soy burger and fry in a pan with a little oil until brown. Place on top of pizza and cook as above.

Fondue

⅔ c.	instant powdered milk
½ tsp.	salt
4 Tb.	cornstarch
1½ c.	water
6 oz.	Swiss cheese
1½ tsp.	paprika
	crackers—Zwieback, Rye Crisp, etc.

Trail directions: In a small deep pan lid mix powdered milk with salt and cornstarch. Add water; stir and simmer until sauce thickens. Slice cheese into thin pieces and add to the sauce along with paprika. Let cheese melt, stirring as little as possible.

Make a double boiler by placing pan containing sauce inside a pot containing hot water. This double boiler arrangement will keep the fondue hot while eating and will also prevent it from burning.

Dip crackers into fondue and eat. Dried beef jerky also is fun to eat with fondue.

Chop Suey

½ c.	white rice
¾ c.	dried beef (see recipe)
2 Tb.	dehydrated sweet bell pepper flakes
2 Tb.	dehydrated minced onion
2 Tb.	dehydrated vegetable flakes
¼ c.	dehydrated mushrooms
1 c.	alfalfa sprouts or diced natural greens (optional)
1 Tb.	miso
¼ tsp.	salt
3 Tb.	oil
3¼ c.	water
⅓ pkg.	sweet and sour sauce

Trail directions: Bring rice, dried beef, onions, mushrooms, pepper, vegetable flakes, greens, miso, salt, oil, and 2¼ c. water to a boil. Simmer with lid for 15 minutes.

In another heating container, combine sweet and sour sauce with 1 c. water. Bring to boil and simmer until thick. Pour over vegetable-rice mixture and serve.

Potato Pancakes

3 Tb.	powdered milk
1 tsp.	onion powder
1 Tb.	parsley or chives
¼ tsp.	black pepper
1 tsp.	salt
3⅓ c.	water
1⅓ c.	potato buds
6 Tb.	margarine
2	eggs (powdered)
½ c.	whole wheat flour
⅔ c.	sliced cheese

Trail directions: Mix powdered milk, onion powder, parsley, pepper and salt with 3⅓ c. water. Bring to a boil. Remove from heat and stir in potato buds. Mix in 2 Tb. of margarine

Mix up powdered eggs in a separate bowl. Add eggs and flour to potato bud mixture, stirring well. Fry potato cakes in an oiled skillet, like pancakes. When turning over, cover each cake with several light strips of cheese.

Hush Puppies

1 c.	cornmeal
⅓ c.	soy flour
⅓ c.	instant powdered milk
¼ c.	sugar
1½ tsp.	onion powder
¾ tsp.	salt
¼ tsp.	black pepper
¼ c.	water
1 c.	vegetable oil

Trail directions: Mix cornmeal, soy flour, powdered milk, sugar, onion powder, salt, pepper, and enough water to form a dough of thick consistency.

Place oil in a deep, narrow pot. Heat oil slowly for several minutes until very hot. Temperature is correct when a small ball made of test batter, dropped into the hot oil, bubbles vehemently. Form batter into ¾ inch balls and place several of them into the hot oil, being sure to cover pot with a lid. Hush puppies are fully cooked when they turn golden and stop their bobbing and float on the oil's surface. Remove from oil, drain, and serve. When finished, cool, oil, strain, and save.

Sauces—Thickeners

Basic White Sauce

3 Tb.	margarine
3 Tb.	white flour
⅓ c.	instant powdered milk
1 c.	water

Trail directions: In a pot melt margarine and bring to a slow boil. Slowly stir in flour and simmer for several minutes. Combine powdered milk with water. Remove pan from heat. Add milk to flour-margarine mixture. Bring to a boil and cook until sauce thickens.

There are many variations to this basic white sauce recipe as follows:

Add ½ c. grated cheese and ½ tsp. paprika, miso or dry mustard.

Add 2 tsp. of curry to margarine before adding rest of basic white sauce's ingredients.

For a brown sauce, substitute 2 beef bouillon cubes for powdered milk. Add pepper and thyme to taste.

Part of a package of instant wine sauce also goes well with the Basic Sauce.

Thickeners

Having a good thickening agent is oftentimes invaluable. Many times the difference between a good satisfying meal and a mediocre one is only a matter of it "sticking to one's ribs."

Cornstarch Thickener

3 Tb.	cornstarch
⅓ c.	instant powdered milk
1 c.	water

Trail directions: Combine cornstarch and powdered milk with a tiny bit of water. Stir to form a paste. Add remaining water, mixing well. Slowly bring to a boil, stirring constantly. Simmer several minutes to desired consistency. Stir into food to be thickened.

Flour Thickener

½ c.   white flour
2 Tb.   non-instant powdered milk
½ c.   water

Trail directions: Combine flour and powdered milk. Add water as in above recipe. Bring the food that needs to be thickened to a boil and then slowly stir in flour sauce.

In a pinch, 2 Tb. instant potatoes also makes a good thickening agent.

Salad Dressing

¼ tsp.   dry mustard
¼ tsp.   garlic powder
¼ tsp.   salt
¼ tsp.   black pepper
1 Tb.   vinegar or lemon juice
4 Tb.   vegetable oil

Trail directions: Mix mustard, garlic powder, salt, and pepper with lemon juice. Pour in a container that can be sealed and shake well. Add oil, shake again, and serve.

This is a recipe for the connoisseur of good foods. In summertime, when there are lots of edible greens, I will bring the above fixings and prepare the dressing. The only ingredient for this dressing that is foreign to most backpack trips is vinegar or lemon juice. Such juices are used in relatively small proportions, though, and may be employed for other dishes too.

Syrup

½ c.   brown sugar
½ c.   water

Trail directions: Mix sugar and water together in a pot. On low heat, bring mixture to a boil and simmer for 10 minutes.

There are many variations to alter this syrup. For instance, boil raisins with the sugar mixture or add a pinch of cinnamon, or even a few ground-up ends of new spruce needles, which makes for an exciting flavor.

Croutons

1 c.   broken up Rye Crisp, Melba Toast, Zwieback,
             or other hard cracker crumbs
4 Tb.   margarine
½ tsp.   onion powder
½ tsp.   garlic powder
1 tsp.   salt

Trail directions: With low heat, saute crackers in margarine until brown. Sprinkle garlic and onion powder plus salt while crackers are cooking.

Croutons go good on a fresh green salad or with many one-pot dinners.

Cereals

Cornmeal Mush

4 c.	water
⅔ c.	cornmeal
2 Tb.	soy grits or 2 Tb soya nuts that have been finely ground up
½ c.	sunflower seeds
½ c.	raisins
1 tsp.	salt
4 Tb.	margarine
⅔ c.	instant powdered milk
2 Tb.	sugar or honey

Cornmeal mush is a good variation for outdoor breakfasts.

Trail directions: Place 4 c. of water, cornmeal, soy grits, sunflower seeds, raisins, and salt into a pot. Bring to a boil and simmer with a lid for 15 minutes, stirring occasionally. When cornmeal has thickened, remove from heat, add margarine, powdered milk, and sugar; serve.

An important variation to cornmeal mush is to fry it. To prepare, in a pot add 1 c. water, milk, raisins, sunflower seeds, soy grits, and sugar; bring to a boil. In a separate bowl, mix 1 c. cornmeal with 1 c. cold water. Stir this cold cornmeal mixture into the boiling water containing the other ingredients. Boil for a full 2 minutes, then simmer with a lid until thickened, about 5-10 more minutes, stirring as little as possible. Set cornmeal aside for at least 2 hours to gel. When cornmeal has completely hardened, cut into thin slices and fry both sides in a well-greased skillet. Fried cornmeal can be ready in the morning if the mush is prepared the night before.

Steve's Hopeful Granola

4 c.	old-fashioned rolled oats
1⅓ c.	whole wheat flakes
1 c.	untoasted wheat germ
1 c.	instant powdered milk
¾ c.	sunflower seeds
⅔ c.	ground up sesame meal
1¼ c.	coconut, preferably unsweetened
1 c.	raisins
1 c.	water
⅔ c.	vegetable oil
1 c.	honey
1 tsp.	pure vanilla extract
1½ tsp.	pure almond extract
½ tsp.	salt

Home directions: In a large bowl combine rolled oats, wheat flakes, wheat germ, milk, sunflower seeds, sesame meal, and coconut.

Boil raisins in 1 c. water for five minutes. Drain and pat dry; add to above mixture.

In a pot simmer vegetable oil, honey, vanilla, almond extract, and salt for several minutes; stir to mix and avoid boiling. Pour liquid over dry ingredients, mixing with a big spoon or your hands until granola is evenly coated.

Place granola into two 9x13 inch pans or several large cookie sheets so that granola is only one-half inch thick; place in a 275° preheated oven for 25 minutes. During this baking time, stir granola in pans every 5 minutes so that it will cook evenly. Granola is done when it just begins to turn a light golden color. Cool granola, then store.

The secret to a successful granola is not to overcook it—i.e., not trying to completely dry out the granola in the oven or letting it become deeply golden. Granola dries out as it cools off.

There are many ways to vary this basic granola recipe. For a more moist granola, use ½ c. oil and ¼ c. water instead of ⅔ c. oil. One may also substitute dried apricots or dates for raisins.

To have a glazed granola, toast oats, wheat flakes, wheat germ, milk, nuts, and raisins for 15-20 minutes in a preheated 200° oven. Use two cookie sheets. Stir every few minutes. In the meantime, prepare oat mixture. As it changes color remove from oven and quickly add the hot liquids and coconut to the dry ingredients (you will hear a sizzling sound). Cool completely before storing.

Familla

2 c.	quick cooking oats
1 c.	rolled wheat or rye flakes
1 c.	whole wheat flour
²/₃ c.	soya nuts
1½ c.	wheat bran
1½ c.	untoasted wheat germ
²/₃ c.	instant powdered milk
1 c.	chopped dried fruit (apricots, peaches, apples)
½ c.	sugar, granulated

Familla is a good-tasting, instant cereal that needs no cooking before eating.

Home directions: Mix instant oats, rolled wheat and whole wheat flour together. Spread on two cookie sheets and lightly toast in a 350° preheated oven for 3-5 minutes. Crush the soya nuts and add them to the remaining ingredients. Mix all ingredients together and store in a plastic bag.

Take as much Familla as you expect you will need on a trip (approximately 1½ c. per person per meal). Familla is best served with milk and allowed to sit for several minutes to thicken.

New Cereal

¼-⅓ c. instant powdered eggs
4 c.   water
2 tsp.   salt
1 c.   quick cooking cereal (Wheatena, Wheat
       Hearts, Ralston, etc.)
2 Tb.   honey or sugar
¼ c.   margarine

Trail directions: Combine powdered eggs with a tiny amount of water. Make a paste and gradually add the remaining amount of 4 c. water and salt. Bring to a boil. Stir in cereal and simmer for five minutes, stirring constantly.

When done, mix in honey and margarine. Serve with milk.

This cereal combination is rather unique. It offers variety in cereal eating and is an easy way to eat eggs. Don't dismiss the recipe until you have actually tried it.

Whole Grain Cereal

1½ c.   cracked wheat
½ c.   raisins
2 tsp.   salt
4½ c.   water
½ c.   instant powdered milk
¼ c.   margarine
2 Tb.   honey or sugar

For those who have never experienced real whole grains, this recipe will be a pleasant surprise.

Trail directions: In a pot add grains, raisins, salt, and water. Bring to a boil, cover, and simmer for 15 minutes. When cooked, slowly stir in powdered milk. Garnish with margarine and honey. Serve.

Cooking time may be shortened by soaking grains the night before in water. Pre-soaked grains only take five minutes of simmering after boiling.

Bulgar is similar to cracked wheat only if it is prepared in 1:2 proportions with water. If one likes a whole grain cereal but wishes to "stretch" the cereal, add 1 c. cracked wheat, ½ c. Wheat Hearts or other commercial cereal, and 5 c. water.

Spreads

H & D Peanut Butter

1 c.	non-hydrogenated peanut butter
½ c.	honey
½ c.	butter or margarine
½ c.	instant powdered milk

Home directions: Melt peanut butter, honey, and margarine together in a pot, being careful not to boil it. Add in powdered milk, mixing well. Pour mixture into a plastic container with a good lid. Spreads well on crackers or dense breads.[1]

Crunchy Nutter Butter

½ c.	non-hydrogenated peanut butter
½ c.	honey
4 Tb.	peanut or vegetable oil
1 ¼ c.	ground up sesame seeds

Home directions: Melt peanut butter and honey together. Stir in oil and sesame seeds, mixing together well. Pour mixture into a plastic container with a good lid. Spreads like thick peanut butter. For a thinner spread, add more oil.

Cake Frosting

⅓-½ c.	white sugar
½ c.	margarine
	pinch of Wylers, instant powdered coffee, cinnamon, or cocoa

Trail directions: Mix sugar and margarine together for several minutes. Depending on taste preference, add in a Tb. of Wylers or other flavoring. Stir in well.

For a special treat, spread frosting over the top of a warm cake that has just been baked. Eat immediately.

---

[1] If employing a peanut butter that's oily, use only ¼ c. margarine or add an extra ½ c. instant powdered milk.

Desserts

Fruit Compote

1	6-oz. pkg. of dried fruit—apples, apricots, etc.
½ c.	brown sugar
1 tsp.	cinnamon
½ tsp.	nutmeg
2½ c.	water
½ c.	white flour
½ c.	whole wheat flour
⅓ c.	instant powdered milk
1 tsp.	baking powder
¼ tsp.	salt

Trail directions: Slice dried fruit into tiny pieces and place in a pot with sugar, cinnamon, nutmeg, and 2 c. water. Bring mixture to a boil and simmer for 10-15 minutes.

Meanwhile, make the covering by mixing flour, powdered milk, baking powder, and salt together. Slowly add in water, one tablespoon at a time, until dough becomes very thick. Roll dough into a ball; then flatten out so it is one-half inch thick and almost the diameter of the pot in which the fruit is boiling.

During the last 5 minutes of cooking the fruit, add dough topping to fruit, laying down gently. Place lid on pot, turn heat down and simmer until dough is cooked (about five minutes).

Garnish top of dough covering with margarine or brown sugar and serve.

It is important that the dough be stiff like bread dough for compote to cook in the required amount of time. One may add raisins, brown sugar, or cinnamon to batter when forming the dough.

Fruit Tarts

6 oz.	dried fruit—apricots, peaches, apples, etc.
¼ c.	brown sugar
1½ tsp.	cinnamon
1 c. + 2 Tb.	water
1 c.	unbleached white flour
½ tsp.	salt
4 Tb.	margarine

Trail directions: Slice fruit into tiny pieces. Put fruit, sugar, 1 tsp. cinnamon, and 1 c. water in a pot. Bring mixture to a boil until fruit sauce thickens, stirring constantly.

Mix flour, ½ tsp. cinnamon and salt together. Melt margarine and stir into flour mixture. Add 2 Tb. water, mixing well. Knead dough with hands for several minutes. Roll out dough into two crusts eight inches in diameter. Place prepared fruit in crusts; fold crusts over onto themselves and pinch edges.

Fry both sides of crusts in an oiled skillet, using low heat and a lid. Serve when lightly browned.

For those desiring an extra sweet crust, sprinkle a little bit of brown sugar on the outside of tart crusts before frying.

Three-Minute Cookies

½ c.	margarine
1 c.	white sugar
¼ c.	powdered cocoa
2 Tb.	instant powdered milk
¼ c.	water
1½ c.	quick cooking rolled oats

Trail directions: In a deep pot, melt margarine. Mix in sugar and cocoa. Combine dry milk with water and add to above ingredients. Bring chocolate syrup to a full rolling boil for 3 minutes. Remove from heat. Stir in rolled oats, mixing until oats are completely coated. Reheat for half a minute, then immediately shape chocolate into small balls and let set on a hard surface until completely cool (about 20 minutes).

Cascade Cake

1 c.	unbleached white flour
1 c.	whole wheat flour
⅔ c.	instant powdered milk
⅓ c.	brown sugar
4 tsp.	baking powder
2 tsp.	cinnamon
½ tsp.	salt
2 Tb.	oil or melted margarine
1 c.	water

Trail directions: Mix flour, powdered milk, brown sugar, baking powder, cinnamon, and salt together. Stir in oil and water, mixing well.

Pour batter into an oiled can or other small container (Sierra cup works great). Place can into a Dutch oven (see chapter on cooking techniques). Cooking time is approximately 10 minutes using hot coals. Recipe yields about five large cakes. For variety add chopped sunflower seeds and raisins when preparing the dough.

Simple No-Bake Pie

2 c.	crushed graham crackers, granola or cookie crumbs
⅓ c.	honey
¼ c.	brown sugar
4 Tb.	margarine
⅔ c.	instant powdered milk
1 small pkg. of instant pudding	
2 c.	water

Trail directions: Combine crumbs of graham crackers, cereal, and/or cookies with honey and brown sugar. Mix margarine in well, stirring for several minutes. Pat crust mixture into a pie tin or frying pan. Cover pan with plastic and place in warm sun for several hours to harden crust. When crust has become stiff, mix up pudding by adding water to powdered milk in a poly-bottle. After milk is prepared, add pudding mix and shake for several minutes. Pour pudding into pie crust and let sit for 15 minutes before eating.

There are lots of other ingredients that can be used for pie crusts. Crushed Rye Crisp or Zweiback, combined cooked brown rice, honey, and sesame seeds are superb. Pie may be topped with instant whipped cream if desired.

Beverages

Caroba

6 Tb.	sugar
2½ c.	instant powdered milk
¾ c.	malted milk
½ c.	carob

Home directions: Combine sugar, powdered milk, and malted milk together. Sift carob, combine with other ingredients and sift once more before storing in a double plastic bag. To use, add 5 Tb. of caroba and enough hot water to make one cup of drink; stir briskly. Recipe makes enough for 12 cups of hot drinks.

Caroba Variations

To one cup of hot caroba add either ½ tsp. cinnamon, nutmeg, or instant freeze-dried coffee, an appropriate strong coffee-tasting herb tea, or part of a vanilla bean. If one desires a super rich drink, add to the hot caroba ¼ c. of powdered milk.

For fudge, combine a quarter cup of cold water to one cup caroba mix, stirring until completely dissolved. Place caroba fudge in a metal cup, cover, and put near a fire. Rotate cup occasionally. Caroba thickens as it becomes hot. Nuts go well in the fudge.

Shakes

1 small	box of instant pudding
1 c.	instant powdered milk
4 c.	water

Trail directions: Combine pudding mix with powdered milk in a one-quart wide-mouth polybottle; shake. Add 2 cups water and shake until completely dissolved. Add remaining water and shake again until completely mixed. Chill in a mountain stream or snowbank if desired.

Trog's Russian Tea

2 c.	orange breakfast drink powder (Tang)
1 c.	plain instant tea
1 qt-size	package lemonade mix, sweetened (Wylers)
1 Tb.	cinnamon
1½ tsp.	ground cloves
¼ c.	white sugar

Home directions: Mix all ingredients together. Store in tightly covered container and take only as much as you expect to drink on your trip (2 Tb. per cup for hot tea). Vary to taste. The tea will be murky because of the spices but it is still great.

Appendix I

Foods Commonly Taken Backpacking

	Calories per lb.	Useable Protein (gm.)
Beverages		
Instant Hot Chocolate (Hershey's)	1760	≈ 26
Instant Breakfast	1680	≈ 49
Tang	1420	0
Wylers Lemonade	1920	0
Cereals		
Familla (commercial)	1750	≈ 32
Granola (commercial)	2080	≈ 29
Granola (recipe)	2120	36
Ralston	1500	≈ 36
Rolled Oats	1760	42
Wheatena (commercial)	1620	≈ 28
Crackers		
Graham Crackers	1720	≈ 16
Rye Crisp	2030	9
Waverly Wafers	1960	≈ 14
Zwieback	1920	≈ 3
Dairy Products		
Butter	3250	0
Cheese, Cheddar	1800	79
Cheese, Swiss	1680	88
Instant Powdered Milk	1630	133
Instant Non-fat Powdered Milk	1650	134
Powdered Eggs	2680	177

Fruits & Vegetables	Calories per lb.	Useable Protein (gm.)
Dates, pitted	1240	≈5
Dried Apples	1250	≈7
Dried Apricots	1180	≈11
Dried Pears	1220	≈7
Onion Flakes	1580	≈19
Potato Buds	1650	≈20
Potatoes, Dehydrated Hash Brown	1730	19
Raisins	1330	≈8

The figures listed in Appendices I & II are obtained from a variety of sources. Every effort has been made to get exact data. When such information was not available, approximations were made. These approximations are conservative and are represented in these appendices by the figure ≈.

Grains & Flour Products	Calories per lb.	Useable Protein (gm.)
Brown Rice, regular	1630	24
Bulgar	1600	31
Cracked Wheat	1640	28
Soy Grits	1710	113
White Rice, instant enriched	1700	24
White Rice, regular enriched	1650	21
Biscuit Mix	1910	≈18
Soy Flour, defatted	1480	130
Wheat Bran	970	40
Wheat Germ	1650	81
Wheat Flakes	1610	30
White Flour, unbleached	1650	≈24
Whole Wheat Flour	1510	36
Egg Noodles, enriched	1760	35
Macaroni, enriched	1670	28
Spaghetti, enriched	1670	≈28
Yellow Corn Meal, enriched, degerminated	1650	≈18

Meats & Meat Substitutes	Calories per lb.	Useable Protein (gm.)
Bac-O-Bits (commercial, soy)	1820	97
Bits O Bacon (commercial)	2120	102
Beef Jerky	1600	≈86
Chicken, canned, boneless	900	64
Corned Beef	960	76
Dried Beef, chipped	920	103
Dried Beef (recipe)	1600	86
Dry Salami	2040	72
GranBurger (commercial, texturized soy)	1680	142
Pemmican (recipe)	2630	≈45

	Calories per lb.	Useable Protein (gm.)
Piem (commercial)	1450	34
Trout, lake, fillets	760	≈66
Tuna fish, canned	1130	89
Vienna Sausage, canned	1090	43
Nuts, Seeds & Legumes		
Cashews	2540	33
Cowpeas (blackeye)	1540	46
Lentils	1540	34
Peanuts, Virginia	2650	51
Peanut Butter	2630	54
Sesame Seeds, whole	2550	44
Soya Nuts (commercial)	2040	107
Sunflower Seeds, hulled	2540	63
White Beans	1500	38

	Ounces	Calories Per Package	Useable Protein (gm.)
Sauces			
Brown Gravy Mix	¾	70	≈1
Cheese Sauce Mix	1¼	170	≈4
Enchilada Sauce Mix	1	90	≈1
Hollandaise Sauce Mix	1-1/8	190	≈2
Spaghetti Sauce Mix	1½	110	≈2
Sloppy Joe Seasoning Mix	1½	120	≈1
Sour Cream Sauce Mix	1¼	190	≈1
Stroganoff Sauce	1¾	190	≈3
Soups			
Chicken Flavor, Noodle Mix	2-5/8	230	≈6
French Onion Mix	2¾	270	≈4
Green Pea with Ham	2¾	240	≈5
Leek Mix	2¾	270	≈2
Mushroom Soup Mix	2¾	290	≈6
Oxtail Soup Mix	2-5/8	270	≈5
Tomato Soup Mix	2¾	270	≈4
Vegetable Soup Mix	2¾	110	≈2
Beef Bouillon, 1 cube	1/8	1	≈1

	Calories per lb.	
Sweets		
Baking Chocolate, semi-sweet	2300	≈13
Cheese Cake, instant	1600	≈26

	Calories Per Package	Useable Protein (gm.)
Hershey's Milk Chocolate Bar	2430	≈22
Hard Candy	1750	0
Honey	1380	0
Jell-O	1790	≈4
Pudding, instant, chocolate	1580	≈6
Sugar, brown	1690	0
Corn Bread Mix	1920	≈8
Date Bar Mix	2190	≈13
Gingerbread Mix	1980	≈13
Snackin' Cake Mix—coconut pecan	2090	≈10

Vegetable Oils
Corn Oil	4010	0
Oleomargarine	3270	≈0

Appendix II

Equivalents

	Weight-Volume Equivalents Per one pound
Apricots, dried	3 c.
Beef, dried	4⅓ c.
Biscuit Mix	3⅔ c.
Bulgar, Cracked Wheat	2⅔ c.
Cashews	3¼ c.
Cheese, Cheddar	2 c.
Chicken, canned	2⅔ c.
Chocolate, baking, semi-sweet	2¼ c.
Cornmeal	3¼ c.
Egg Noodles	6¼ c.
Famila	3⅔ c.
GranBurger	5 c.
Granola	4 c.
Honey	1⅓ c.
Hot Chocolate, instant	3¾ c.
Lentils	2½ c.
Macaroni	4 c.
Milk, instant, powdered	4¾ c.
Oleomargarine	2 c.
Pemmican	2⅓ c.
Peanut Butter	1¾ c.
Peanuts	2 c.
Potato Flakes	4½ c.
Raisins	4⅓ c.
Rice—instant, white	9 c.
regular, white	3⅔ c.
Sesame Seeds	3¼ c.
Sugar, Brown	2 c.
Sunflower Seeds	3½ c.
Wheat Bran	9 c.
Wheat Germ	4 c.
Wheatena	4 c.
Whole Wheat Flour	3¾ c.
Beans, white	2⅔ c.
Tang	2½ c.
Tuna fish	2⅓ c.
Vegetable Oil	2 c.

*2 oz. cheese = 1 c. grated cheese

Appendix III

Individual Recipe Nutrition Information

	Ounces	Calories	Useable Protein (gm.)
Breads			
Portuguese Honey Bread	45	5140	89
Logan Bread	43.6	5090	88
Pain au Chocolat	45	5160	86
Cherry-Berry Tea Bread	31.4	4220	80
Pumpkin Bread	30.8	4500	88
Golden Carrot Cake	40.4	4540	87
Banana Nut Bread	33.6	4250	87
Fresh Corn Bread	12.3	1210	33
Bannoc	12.6	1240	28
Cathy's Biscuits	12.5	1450	29
H & D Pancakes	13.2	1310	35
Bars & Candies			
No Bake Fudge	28.2	3490	23
Coffee Toffee Bars	31.4	4870	52
Breakfast Bars	31.4	3730	53
Flapjacks	20.4	2850	33
Scotch Shortbread	20	3150	35
Sesame Bombs	18.6	1506	31
Sesame Crunch	10.4	1070	10
Peanut Brittle	34.8	3840	55
Ohm Balls	16.1	2180	33
Gunk	18.2	3040	79
Marzipan	17.1	2410	15
Gorp	22.8	3090	55
Apricot Leather	30.4	900	8
Meat			
Dried Beef	9.5	800	≈50
Tak's Beef Jerky	14.2	1190	≈75
Pemmican	17.7	2570	≈50
Dinners			
Tangy Rice	17.8	1910	48
Sea of Cortez	13.5	1530	31
Rice and Milk	21	2350	41
Arroz con Queso	20.8	2230	31
Rice Pilaff	13.8	1590	23
Oxtail Soup	20.2	2090	36

	Ounces	Calories	Useable Protein (gm.)
Chicken-Rice Curry	21	2390	44
Beef Stroganoff	14	1510	39
Chicken Noodle Soup	17.6	2010	57
Macaroni & Cheese	14.2	1730	50
Chili Mac	9.4	1080	42
Lentils Of Course	14.6	1660	44
Lentil Stew	13.4	1330	26
Chipped Beef	19.3	2200	43
Tamale Pie	11.3	1100	20
Chapades	12.5	1490	31
Enchiladas	19.2	2110	41
Quesadillas	14.4	1740	41
French Onion Soup	10.1	1150	36
Cheese Blitz	19.9	2480	59
Spaghetti	18.8	2340	29
Skillet Pizza	22	2730	43
Fondue	13.2	1360	52
Potato Pancakes	10.1	1370	29
Hush Puppies	11.1	1210	20
Chop Suey	13.4	1240	22
Chinese Cuisine	7	590	16
Sauces—Thickeners			
Basic White Sauce	3.6	410	11
Corn Starch Thickener	2.6	210	8
Flour Thickener	2.5	230	7
Salad Dressing	3.0	120	0
Syrup	3.9	410	0
Croutons	5.9	760	0
Cereals			
Whole Grain Cereal	16.8	1970	36
Steve's Hopeful Granola	47.1	6220	105
Familla	37.8	3300	94
Cornmeal Mush	14.2	1551	31
New Cereal	8.2	1120	19
Spreads			
H & D Peanut Butter	21.1	2920	84
Crunchy Peanut Butter	17.8	2620	55
Cake Frosting	6.6	1080	0
Desserts			
Fruit Compote	15.2	1310	16
Cascade Cake	11.5	1140	33
Fruit Tart	13.9	1440	9
Simple No-Bake Pie	19.8	2066	27
Three-Minute Cookies	17.9	2170	14

	Ounces	Calories	Useable Protein (gm.)
Beverages			
Caroba	9.5	1210	28
Shakes	9	680	44 up
Trog's Russian Tea	18.9	1710	0

Appendix IV

Iodinating Water

Water purification using iodine crystals is an effective way to destroy amoebic cysts, enteroviruses, and other disease-producing organisms.[1] Equipment needed includes a one-ounce clear plastic bottle with a leak-proof lid and a small amount of USP-grade resublimed iodine crystals purchased at a local chemical supply store. A thermometer is optional.

Weigh four to eight grams of the pure iodine crystals and add to the glass bottle; fill with water and shake continuously for one minute. Allow the undissolved crystals to settle on the bottle's bottom. The iodine solution in the bottle is what one adds to the water which needs to be treated; the crystals themselves remain on the bottom of the bottle. The amount of concentrated solution used to treat infected water depends on the temperature of the iodine solution. And, the temperature of the water being treated determines how long the treated water needs to stand before it is safe to be consumed.

For example, if the temperature of the iodine solution is 68°F, one adds 13cc of iodine solution to one quart of water. And if the quart of water is 68° F, one must wait thirty minutes before all the harmful contaminants are destroyed and the water can be safely consumed. Approximately half an hour would be needed with the same strength solution and the water temperature at 50° F. With especially dirty contaminated water, doubling the recommended solution will ensure complete contamination-free water.

100

One can use the cap of the iodine solution bottle as a crude measuring device provided one has previously measured how many cc's the cap contains. After each purification, remake the concentrated solution by adding additional water to the iodine bottle. Four to eight grams of iodine crystals is enough to purify 1,000 quarts of water.

Amounts of iodine used in this water purification technique have low toxicity. Persons with specific iodine sensitivities or thyroid problems, though, ought to use another treatment process. Poisoning effects by accidentally swallowing some or all of the iodine crystals is unlikely, for all reported fatalities involved 15 grams or more of iodine.

---

[1]See *Off Belay*, Vol. 33, pp. 23-24, June 1977, and "Water Disinfection in the Wilderness," Fredrick Kahn and Barbara Visscher, *Western Journal of Medicine*, May 1975, for further elaboration in iodinating techniques.

Bibliography

Anonymous, *Amino-Acid Content of Foods and Biological Data on Protein*, Food Policy and Food Science Service, Nutrition Division in FAO of the U.N., Rome, 1970.

——, *Off Belay*, Dec. 1973, No. 12, pp. 6-26, Renton, Washington.

——, *Recommended Dietary Allowances*, National Academy of Sciences, Washington, D.C., 1974.

——, Composition of Foods, *Agricultural Handbook*, No. 8, United States Department of Agriculture, Washington D.C., 1963.

Bowes and Church, *Food Values of Proportions Commonly Used*, J. B. Lippincott Co., Philadelphia, Pennsylvania, 1972.

Bunnelle, H. and Sarvis, S., *Cooking for Camp and Trail*, Sierra Club, San Francisco, California, 1976.

Eward, Ellen B., *Recipes for a Small Planet*, Ballantine Books, New York, New York, 1973.

Fletcher, Colin, *The New Complete Walker*, Second Edition, A. A. Knopf, Inc., New York, New York, 1977.

Kahn, F., and Visscher, B., Drs., "Water Disinfection in the Wilderness,"*The Western Journal of Medicine*, pp. 122-5, San Francisco, California, May 1975.

Kleiner, I., and Orten, J., *Biochemistry*, Mosby Co., St. Louis, Missouri, 1962.

Kraus, Barbara, *Dictionary of Protein*, the New American Library, Inc., New York, New York, 1972.

Lappe, Frances Moore, *Diet for a Small Planet*, Ballantine Books, New York, New York, 1973.

Macmaniman, Gen, *Dry It—You'll Like It!*, Evergreen Printing Co., Fall City, Washington, 1974.

Manning, Harvey, ed., *Mountaineering, The Freedom of the Hills*, The Mountaineers, Third edition, Seattle, Washington, 1974.

Pallister, Nancy, ed., *NOLS Cookery*, National Outdoor Leadership School, Lander, Wyoming, 1974.

Robinson, Corinine Hodgen, *Fundamentals of Normal Nutrition*, Macmillan Publishing Co., New York, New York, 1973.

Stefansson, Vihjalmur, *The Fat of the Land,* The Macmillan
Publishing Co., New York, N.Y., 1957.

Van Liere, Edward J. and Stockney, J. C., *Hypoxia,* University of Chicago Press, Chicago, Illinois, 1963.

Index